BY BRINK BILL CAHAN JANET DED

KRUEGER TIM LARSEN DAVE MASON NORITO SH

OSEPH AND NANCY ESSEX CARIN G

T KEVIN KRUEGER DAVE MASON

LEY JACQUES KOEWEIDEN JAMIE K

LMANN-LEAVITT KEVIN KRUEGER TIM LARSEN D

ANN TRAVER MICHAEL VANDERBY

MASON NORITO SHINMURA JIM ANTONOPOULO

BURAK BIZER GABY BRINK BILL CA

TIM LARSEN DAVE MASON NORITO SHINMURA J

VANESSA ECKSTEIN JOSEPH AND N

IN KRUEGER TIM LARSEN DAVE MASON NORITO

HART ALEXANDER ISLEY JACQUE

N-LEAVITT KEVIN KRUEGER TIM LARSEN DAVE M

S OEHLER GUILLERMO STEIN ANN

MASTERS OF DESIGN
CORPORATE BROCHURES

ROCKPORT

First published in the United States of America by
Rockport Publishers, a member of
Quayside Publishing Group
100 Cummings Center
Suite 406-L
Beverly, Massachusetts 01915-6101
Telephone: (978) 282-9590
Fax: (978) 283-2742
www.rockpub.com

Library of Congress Cataloging-in-Publication Data

Adams, Sean.
  Masters of design : corporate brochures : a collection of the
most inspiring corporate communications designers in the world
/ Sean Adams.
      p. cm.
  Includes bibliographical references and index.
  ISBN-13: 978-1-59253-546-0
  ISBN-10: 1-59253-546-1
1. Brochures--Design. 2. Industrial design coordination.
I. Title. II. Title: Corporate brochures. III. Title: Collection
of the most inspiring brochure designers in the world.
  Z246.5.B76A33 2009
  741.6--dc22

                                        200902133
                                        CIP

ISBN-13: 978-1-59253-546-0
ISBN-10: 1-59253-546-1

10 9 8 7 6 5 4 3 2 1

Design: AdamsMorioka, Inc.
Printed in Singapore

SEAN ADAMS

MASTERS OF DESIGN: CORPORATE BROCHURES

A COLLECTION OF THE MOST INSPIRING CORPORATE COMMUNICATIONS DESIGNERS IN THE WORLD

BEVERLY MASSACHUSETTS

ROCKPORT PUBLISHERS

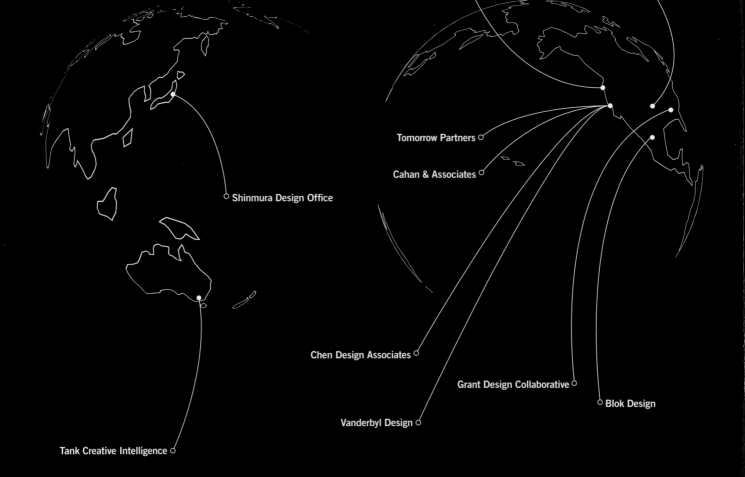

Shinmura Design Office

Tomorrow Partners

Cahan & Associates

Chen Design Associates

Grant Design Collaborative

Blok Design

Vanderbyl Design

Tank Creative Intelligence

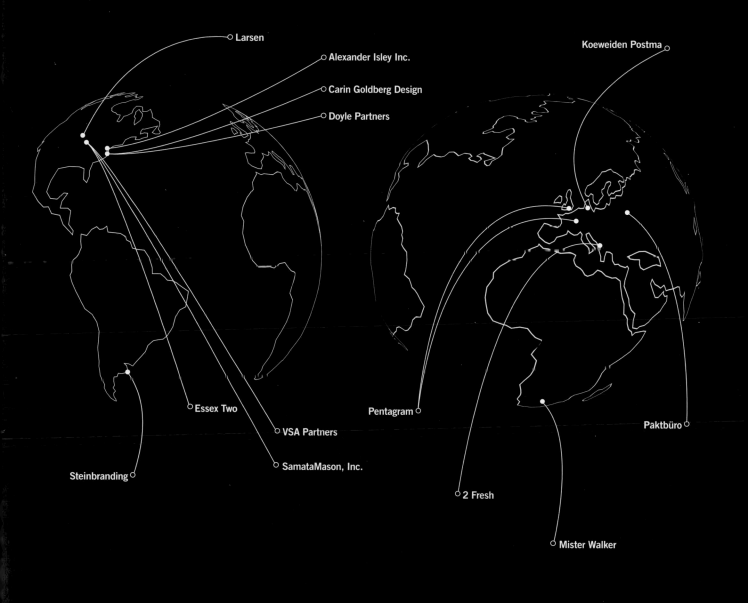

Larsen

Alexander Isley Inc.

Carin Goldberg Design

Doyle Partners

Koeweiden Postma

Essex Two

VSA Partners

SamataMason, Inc.

Steinbranding

Pentagram

Paktbüro

2 Fresh

Mister Walker

A clear and proprietary message and point of view are a critical part of a company's success. This can be achieved in many ways, some visual, others operational. A strong identity is the foundation. The entirety of a company's communications completes the structure. Fifty years ago, the communications package included print materials, advertising, and, perhaps, television. Today, the venues to disseminate a message are not only vast but are constantly shifting. Designers now articulate the message with booklets, annual reports, brochures, posters, websites, mobile devices, motion, and ever-increasing new technologies.

A key point today is the prevalence of digital and web communication. Why is print important? Is print relevant? Are we seeing the end of print? These are all questions that are asked by the design and business world. As evidenced by the twenty masters in this book, print is alive and well, more relevant, and by no means disappearing. The audience is using other technologies to find information, but an object maintains an emotional connection as an artifact we hold and keep. There may be fewer pieces being produced in print, but the pieces being made are even more important. It is not enough to slap together an acceptable booklet. That booklet must now hold all of the client's qualities and messages and impart them in the strongest way possible.

There is a process that a viewer uses to access information online. It follows like this: go to a company's website, click on the appropriate navigation, drill down deeper, find the information, stop. This is useful and efficient to identify facts and understand a question. The process to access information in print is different: pick up the publication, leaf through the pages, notice other messages, find the answer, hold the object and experience an emotional connection and sense of ownership. If a designer's goal is to communicate the breadth and depth of a client's abilities, as well as a clear personality, the object—the publication—becomes a critical vehicle. It may serve as a "gateway" to the website, but it is the artifact that will sit on someone's desk or bookshelf. It will be handled and the texture of the paper will become a tactile experience. And the viewer may stumble across an idea they weren't looking for while glancing through the other parts of the publication.

In the same way that a strong identity cannot make a poor company better, strong print publications cannot be the only vehicle for a company to succeed. The combination of a strong logo and identity system, superb print collateral, and the highest quality of digital communications can make a very good company spectacular. The masters in this book share the common trait of working with a company to pull together all of these aspects and combine them with operational and human resource issues to propel their clients into areas beyond their expectations.

THINK

THINK

Dana Arnett   Jamie Koval

VSA Partners • Chicago, Illinois, USA ●

Working as a team can be difficult and lead to diluted ideas and solutions that everyone can support. The most original ideas are quickly lost when multiple decision-makers need to agree. VSA Partners does not have this problem. It is not the kind of firm where everyone always agrees and sees the world in exactly the same way. But it is their differences that are at the heart of their success. Partner Dana Arnett's first impulse on a project is to understand the business implications of what the designer is doing for the client. A designer needs a critical understanding of the client's business objectives. "Gaining knowledge about the client's business leads to an understanding of what will best serve them." Arnett says.

OPPOSITE AND
PAGES 10–11
The *2007 Annual Review* is one of many projects VSA has created for IBM. This collaboration ranges from brand strategy and design to key investor, partner, and corporate communications. VSA's goal is to infuse the IBM brand with clarity, humanity, and wit, from print and Internet-based tools to inspirational brand presentations for business groups companywide.

"It's not enough to make pretty things—these pretty things must be ever more effective," says Arnett. Good clients know how to leverage design. They value creativity for its ability to make them more competitive. "Competing in a vastly commoditized world means creating value quicker. We've been lucky to work with some of the best companies. They are out front with their marketing, and are well aware of what they need to do to stay ahead of the competition. Other clients are going through significant changes to be able to move forward in a global economy. Our strategy has broadened and deepened with our clients," Arnett adds.

VSA has had clients insist they need collateral and printed brochures for a sales force that must go in front of customers. Traditionally, people like to interact with verbal and visual information. At these times, VSA Partners is ahead of the client in terms of knowledge and experience with using new communication methods. Rather than rejecting the client's request, they work to understand its genesis and find a solution. "They may be dealing with a legacy sales approach," Arnett says, "As designers, we need to see if it's possible to create something that's going to be successful given the client's current practices."

C Level

Koval insists that a key component to success with corporate communications is the decision-maker. The most challenging part of all projects is getting to the top. "The closer you are to the 'C suite,' the more a piece is a true reflection of a company's leadership," he says. "Begin at the highest level and have a clear sense of where he or she is going with the organization." Once this vision has been established, the designer can leverage that information within the client's organization. He continues, "This allows you to shape your story. It also lets you cleanly get through the organization and decide what is important and what isn't. It helps in preserving the point of view and drives concepts." It rarely works when a designer starts at the bottom and tries to push upwards.

For Arnett, it is impossible to succeed without a strong sense of purpose. This can be the result of the writing, the media, or the design. The blogosphere is only about purpose. Information is circulated to influence others. People blog because they have an opinion and they care. As human beings, we like to interact, and we have an appetite for information about our interests. "The success of Google is beyond its functionality. Their early success defined searching the web," says Arnett, "The simplicity and approach, built on the needs of both businesses and consumers, speaks

to purpose completely. Google's competitors don't know how to balance the needs of both business and consumer audiences. They try to be all things for everyone, and that is nearly impossible."

At VSA Partners, designers are encouraged to learn about business. A fundamental appreciation and a desire to understand the client's business can be the most exciting part of a project. It is a permission slip that allows creativity to bloom. For Koval and Arnett, understanding a client's business is a catalyst for design and storytelling to flourish. "The young designers who are the least successful are the ones who believe that design, and design alone, can solve problems. They think of design only on a craft level. Success is slim in those instances," says Arnett. It isn't critical for a designer to take business courses, but if he or she is getting into the world of corporate communications, it is necessary to know about business. That's a fundamental factor for success. It is VSA Partners' multiarmed process and intuitive mindset that continues to create work that is not only beautiful and surprising, but yields business results.

from complex

to manageable

from many

to one

L
ALIGN
N
K

>> *OF ALL THE MEDIUMS of personal or professional
communication, letters hold special value to both sender
and recipient. In contrast to email, phone conversations and
even face-to-face conversations, letters are less immediate —
but they are more rare. In fact, their rarity adds to their
impact: They require more effort to create, and thus demand
more attention. They convey more importance and greater
permanence. They can be more formal. And they typically
have a specific purpose, with a specific response in mind.*

>> *For all these reasons, letters are — literally — wrapped gifts.
They present the products of our thinking and, often,
matters of the heart. So, when considering how to present
yourself, your ideas or your desires to someone, consider
whether YOUR EXPRESSION DESERVES MORE
substance than just hitting a send button, and ask: "Is what
I need to communicate more valuable on paper?"*

2/3

LEFT AND PAGES 16–17
VSA's reintroduction of Strathmore writing paper to the identity design market, following the brand's acquisition by Mohawk Fine Papers, emphasizes a bold and elegant aesthetic designed to appeal to independent designers, design firms, and corporate design departments. The *Dear* promotion builds a market-place association between Strathmore and writing.

2

WHAT MODE *are you in?*

8/9

7

INSIST *on action.*

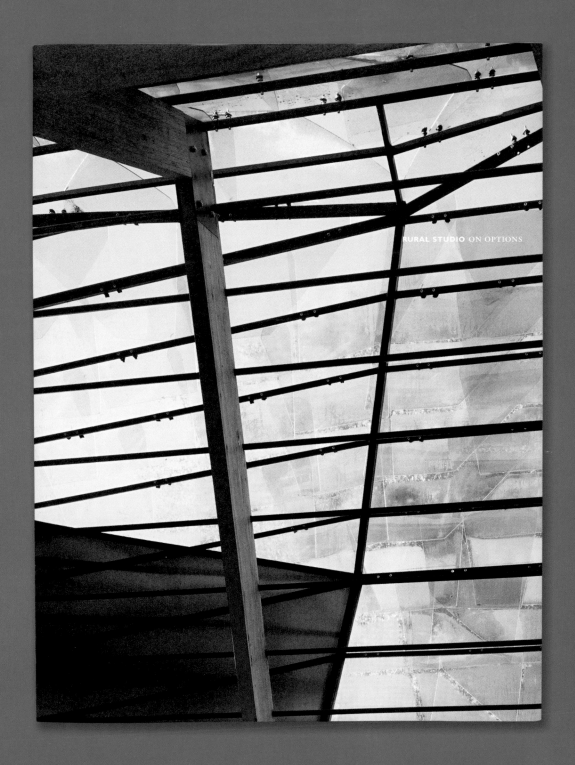

RURAL STUDIO ON OPTIONS

ABOVE AND OPPOSITE
The "On Options" magalog series produced by Mohawk Fine Papers reaches the graphic design community, explaining the creative choices made by leading practitioners in adjacent design fields. The work of these true originals includes an inside look at creative choices, from inspiration to implementation. Among the people and groups featured are the community-based architecture of Alabama's Rural Studio and the Adidas footwear design team.

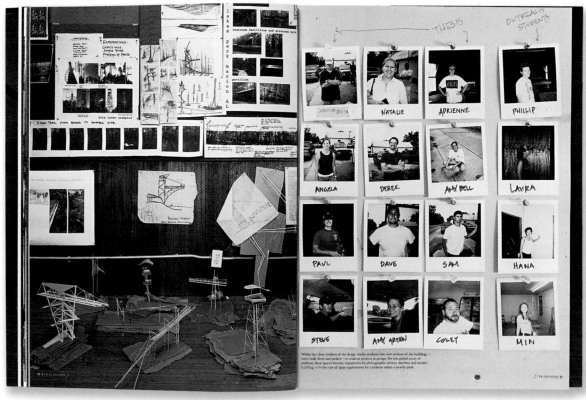

THESIS

OUTREACH STUDENTS

NATALIE

ADRIENNE

PHILLIP

ANGELA

DEREK

AMY BELL

LAURA

PAUL

DAVE

SAM

HANA

STEVE

AMY GREEN

COLEY

MIN

Within the close confines of the design studio, students take over sections of the building—every wall, floor and surface—to work on projects in groups. For this global array of students, these spaces become repositories for photographic surveys, sketches and model-building. At the rear of these explorations for a lookout within a nearby park.

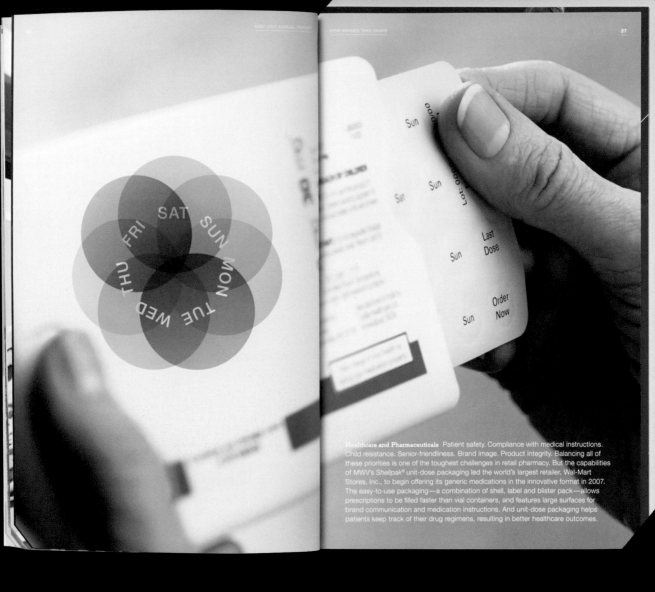

Healthcare and Pharmaceuticals Patient safety. Compliance with medical instructions. Child resistance. Senior-friendliness. Brand image. Product integrity. Balancing all of these priorities is one of the toughest challenges in retail pharmacy. But the capabilities of MWV's *Shellpak*® unit-dose packaging led the world's largest retailer, Wal-Mart Stores, Inc., to begin offering its generic medications in the innovative format in 2007. The easy-to-use packaging—a combination of shell, label and blister pack—allows prescriptions to be filled faster than vial containers, and features large surfaces for brand communication and medication instructions. And unit-dose packaging helps patients keep track of their drug regimens, resulting in better healthcare outcomes.

The Top 3 Rules

1. Make a compelling case.
2. Help define the company.
3. Develop a visual and verbal language that supports it.

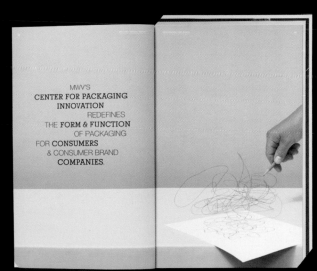

It's not enough to make pretty things."

—Dana Arnold

ABOVE

To underscore MWV's strategic transformation from packaging supplier to creative partner, its 2007 annual report is multidimensional—literally. The body of the book is designed in stepped message and aesthetic. This type of multifaceted storytelling reflects the way MWV—formerly MeadWestvaco—thinks about packaging design and the solutions it creates for its consumer brand partners.

GALLUP

MANAGEMENT JOURNAL

SUMMER 2001 • DATA-DRIVEN MANAGEMENT INTELLIGENCE • WWW.GALLUPJOURNAL.COM

COVER STORY

THE LOYAL CUSTOMER

THE CARE AND FEEDING OF YOUR MOST VALUABLE BUSINESS ASSET

PLUS The HUMAN SIDE of BRAND. LEADERSHIP'S many MOLDS. ZERO in on SOLUTIONS to CUSTOMER COMPLAINTS. HOW a SO-SO ECONOMY AFFECTS a PRESIDENTIAL ELECTION. WHO'S HAPPIER on the JOB: MEN or WOMEN? PROOF THAT TRAINING PAYS OFF. 60-PLUS YEARS of DATA on RELIGIOUS FERVOR

Carin Goldberg

Carin Goldberg Design • Brooklyn, New York, USA

Thomas Edison said, "Vision without execution is hallucination." The design world is littered with people who talk about strategy, use terms such as, "paradigm shift," and are good at producing volumes of data. Unfortunately, much of this work stops there. Nothing is designed or produced. Carin Goldberg is the stellar example that keeps the design profession grounded. She will not succumb to meaningless verbiage and the buzzword *du jour.* Goldberg is pragmatic and straightforward. She will tell the client what they need to know, and she will tell it honestly. Her work is as levelheaded as her personal style. It is not difficult to access. It is not frilly or fussy. It is not self-serving or overbearing. It is lucid, playful, coherent, and crystal clear.

OPPOSITE
The Gallup Management Journal, created for the noted research company, is based on editor/author Jessica Korn's concept that companies can be humanitarian, holistic, and sustainable and still make money. The publication focuses on making more with less and building customer loyalty through these good corporate citizenship practices.

GALLUP
MANAGEMENT JOURNAL

A FRESH LOOK AT TEAMS
In the best work groups, individuals blossom.
ALSO: WHY TO SAY YOU'RE SORRY. ON THE IMPORTANCE OF ORDINARY THINGS.

GALLUP
MANAGEMENT JOURNAL

Making the Most of What You Have
When to Be Good at Many Things Rather Than Best at One • How JetBlue Does More Where It Matters
ALSO: DON'T JUST TACK YOUR MISSION STATEMENT ON THE DOOR

GALLUP
MANAGEMENT JOURNAL

ONE RINGY-DINGY
IS ALL IT TAKES TO LOSE A LIFELONG CUSTOMER
PLUS: DON'T PROMOTE STAR WORKERS • MANAGING EXTREME TALENT • WHY WORKPLACE PALS BOOST PROFIT.

GALLUP
MANAGEMENT JOURNAL

THE POWER OF FEEDBACK
HOW EMPLOYEE INPUT CAN DRIVE YOUR BOTTOM LINE

WHAT'S IN A
CHAIR?
Adjustable, flexible, durable: The qualities companies want in employees are expressed in the office chairs they procure.

THINK BIG, ACT
SMALL
When it comes to worker engagement, size matters.

THEY'VE GOT
GAME
IF YOU DON'T SCORE A SPOT ON A PROFESSIONAL BASKETBALL TEAM, TRY SALES.

WHO
CARED?
After September 11, worker morale depended on corporate response to the tragedy.

Attention
POINT.

CUSTOMERS
CAN ALWAYS HANG UP.

A CUSTOMER TUNES OUT ALL OTHER BRANDS.

PROFILES IN SALES
COURAGE
What defines the great salesperson in the information age?

1960s	2000s

THE VIEW FROM "C" LEVEL
BUDDY SYSTEM
THE COLLECTIVE ADVANTAGE
HOW TO HIRE THE CRÈME DE LA CRÈME
DON'T PROMOTE YOUR STARS
TUNING UP YOUR TALENT ENGINE
IT'S STILL A MAN'S WORLD
THINK BIG, ACT SMALL
WHO'S ANSWERING THE PHONE?
GRASPING INTANGIBLES
THE FORCE THAT CREATED THE BOMB

WE HAVE A FEW NUMBERS THAT MIGHT INTEREST
YOU
IF YOU HIRE BASED ON CLEAR TALENT DEFINITIONS, WORKPLACE PERFORMANCE WILL MEASURABLY IMPROVE. BUT YOU NEED BETTER DEFINITIONS.

GALLUP
Management Journal
Fall 2000 | POWERFUL DATA FOR MANAGING PEOPLE AND BRANDS
Making Customers More LOYAL
How Lessons from One Industry Apply to Others

WHEN
CUSTOMERS EXPERIENCE PROBLEMS—A SERVICE GLITCH OR A FAULTY PRODUCT—A SURPRISING THING HAPPENS

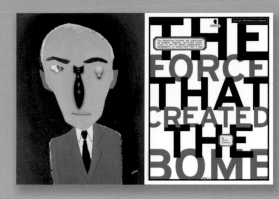

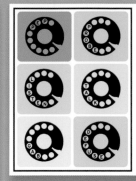

LEFT AND OPPOSITE
Covers and spreads for the
*The Gallup Management
Journal* work cohesively
with content to prove that
a more humanistic busi-
ness approach is viable
and credible by measuring
the ideas using research
and polling data. The
Journal is a marriage of
tangible data, Korn's ideas
and Goldberg's playful
and lively touch to create an
accessible communication.

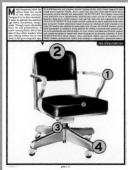

ABOVE AND OPPOSITE
Each year since 2003, a long-standing influential design instructor from The School of Visual Arts in New York is asked to design and edit *The Senior Library*, a project that uniquely reflects and incorporates the talent and the spirit of both the book designer, as well as the graduating seniors whose work is highlighted throughout the book. When it was Goldberg's turn, she asked all seniors to create black-and-white, high-contrast drawings of their profiles, hands, and eyes. From there, using all of the drawings, Goldberg created patterns, collages, and single images. These images became the core idea for the project both visually and editorially.

There are few designers who will state emphatically that they are corporate communications designers. Goldberg is no different. She began her career at CBS Television, CBS Records, and Atlantic Records before founding Carin Goldberg Design in 1982. This entrance into the professional design world colors her work. There are many points of entry, many ways of thinking about corporate communications. A designer can approach the problem as an information design issue, or as a visual exercise, or as a glossy cover-up. Even with the dourest content, Goldberg injects a level of entertainment.

"I use the same approach with any design project. It's problem solving," says Goldberg. She is aware that the end user is critical. "It's important to determine how to make a piece resonate with the intended audience."

Hearts and Minds

Goldberg begins every project with a set of vital questions, "How do I get someone, the right someone, to notice or care? How to I get to their hearts? Then to their minds?" These are not esoteric or feel-good issues. But is this possible with purely digital means? For Goldberg, print is still the most comfortable and nostalgic medium. While she agrees that digital media is becoming increasingly

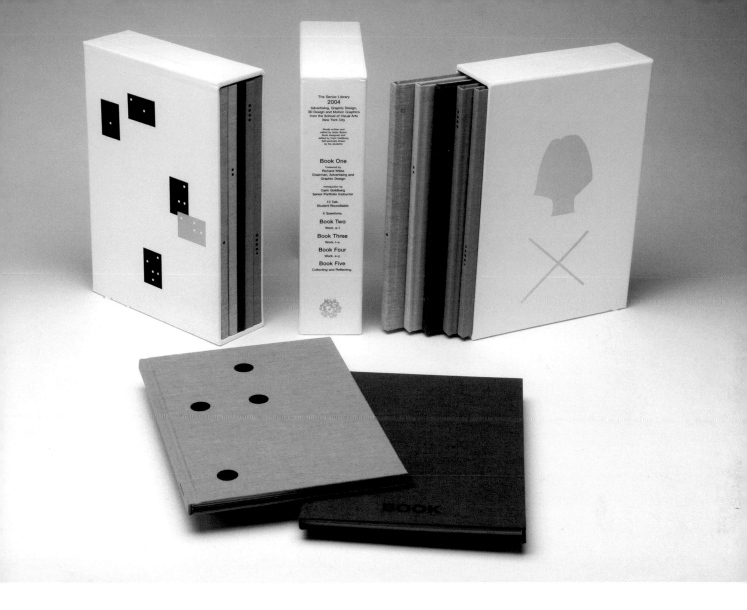

comfortable, and for some audiences preferred, Goldberg maintains that there is a unique personal experience of handling a printed page. "I came into this business never dreaming that we'd be at the point we are today," says Goldberg, "Like many designers, I have struggled with the pressure to have to adapt to digital media and its inevitability. Plus, the medium or technology should not be the obstacle to good ideas and good design. But lately I'm less concerned and I've decided that I'm too old to panic about digital technology and the future of print. I've had my chance to make a decent body of work in print over the last thirty years. I'm off the hook—sort of."

Each client has, or should have, a distinct message. Goldberg takes this one step further and provides a point of view that she and the client will then articulate. The philosophy that defines the client defines the design. This is not equivalent to a dull and plain message. "Being consistent doesn't have to be boring. The design should reflect the client's philosophical ideas and I initially encourage them to inform the general psychology of the project," says Goldberg. In the context of a publication, her process is an exploration that defines the philosophy, and then clarifies that message. Each version is a more refined articulation. She explains, "It's a challenge, but the message will get clearer and clearer with each step."

Do the Right Thing

Goldberg's experience with the *Gallup Management Journal* is a snapshot of her method. The journal is based on editor/author Jessica Korn's concept that companies can be humanitarian, holistic, and sustainable and still make money. Goldberg collaborated with Korn to articulate this vision for Gallup, the research company. The solution created a publication that focused on making more with less and building customer loyalty through these good corporate citizenship practices. Goldberg says, "Jessica's vision was a completely different approach to running a company. Gallup wanted

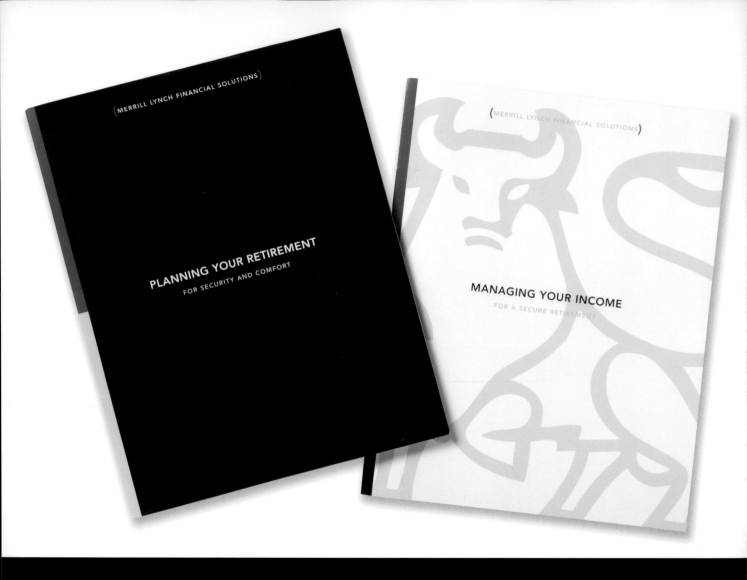

(MERRILL LYNCH FINANCIAL SOLUTIONS)

PLANNING YOUR RETIREMENT
FOR SECURITY AND COMFORT

(MERRILL LYNCH FINANCIAL SOLUTIONS)

MANAGING YOUR INCOME
FOR A SECURE RETIREMENT

"Take a holistic approach to life; you can't separate being a good designer from being a good person."

—**Carin Goldberg**

ABOVE AND OPPOSITE
The booklet for Merrill
Lynch Financial Solutions
explains the process for
retirement planning and
management of wealth.
Typically complex and
daunting, Goldberg
simplifies the steps with
straightforward language

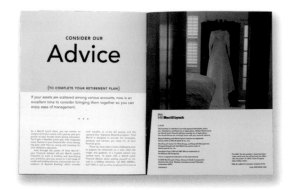

IN THIS ISSUE:
Schooling
Young Investors
**Preserving Your
Family Business
In the Eurozone**

citigroup Pb

EXCLUSIVELY FOR CLIENTS OF THE CITIGROUP PRIVATE BANK ✳ FEBRUARY 2004

**LOCATION, LOCATION,
LOCATION**
**HOW TOP INVESTORS
MASTER THE
REAL ESTATE MARKET**

ABOVE AND OPPOSITE
Citigroup Private Bank
creates innovative
strategies for the world's
wealthiest and most influential families, providing
exclusive access to Citi's
global reach. Goldberg
designed the Citibank
PB magazine to be
entertaining and flexible.
Each issue has a distinc-
tive appearance, but
retains a unified spirit
with the other issues.

to prove that her ideas were viable and credible by measuring the ideas using research and polling data. "The *Journal* was an interesting marriage of tangible data and Korn's ideas about implementing a new, more humanist approach to business. She rejected formulaic communication strategies so many companies employ." The publication is approachable, not esoteric. Goldberg created a look and feel that the client coined "American."

"It's not easy in a large and conservative corporate structure to do adventurous work," says Goldberg. The publication had the right pulse for the subject matter. "For me, it's about paying attention, and exploiting any opportunity to solve the problem with intelligence, wit, and an element of surprise," she notes. "I have to assess the advantages and disadvantages of the situation by getting to know my client's fears, reservations, or expectations. I go with what feels right and true." Goldberg designed a beautiful wood type logotype, but the client wanted to use their corporate font, Times Roman. If Goldberg had persisted in trying to use the wood type, she

may have been seen as myopic or, bluntly, a pain in the ass. Goldberg agreed to lose the wood type, and as a result garnered goodwill. "You just have to know which battles are worth fighting and when the path of least resistance and avoiding conflict is prudent. I knew that if I forced my hand on the logotype I would potentially lose the interior design of the book and the trust from my client necessary for the duration of the project."

Less Stuff

Sustainability is another buzzword in our culture now. It is easily tossed around in meetings, but rarely internalized. As a designer, Goldberg feels that it is important to consider it, but finds many designers don't know how to deal with sustainable practices. "I think we make too many things in general. We should consider making less stuff," she says. At the AIGA Minnesota Design Camp, Goldberg did a lecture called *Truth*. She explored what truth is in graphic design. Goldberg impressed the need to avoid using our skills and talents for people and companies that resist positive change and actions. She said, "We can support things like sustainability by choosing to work with like-minded clients. It's more than just choosing recycled paper."

Goldberg has taught at the School of Visual Arts for twenty years. This is an expression of her commitment to design and the community. Her advice to students is a clue to the skills she possesses. The advice is as direct and clear as her work:

Pay attention and listen.

Have a good idea.

Hang out with the right people, and have your days filled with encouragement and inspiration. Take a holistic approach to life; you can't separate being a good designer from being a good person.

zettai H na syousetsu

Hanamura mangetsu / Fukumori nanmei

Amakasu Ririko / Hinata Tomogi

kongetsuno gokujou Tenohira no monogatari kurumatani cyokitsu

okuda Hideo

「Tokyo hatsu New York keiyu」

suzuki koji

Hachinenburi no horror cyohen

「edge・cityj」

yamada Tosuke / Yamamoto Fumio / kakuda Michiyo

Eiga 「chakusin ari」

Yousiidai No.002
角川書店

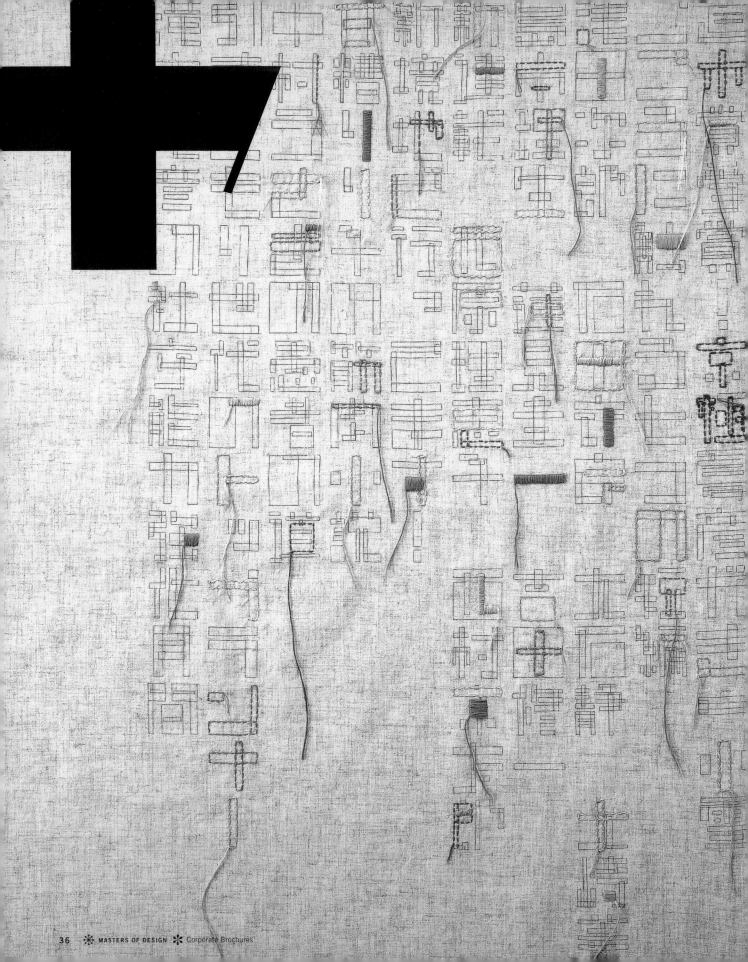

GEORGE
DANGERFIELD
THE
STRANGE
DEATH OF
LIBERAL
ENGLAND

S

Justus Oehler

● **Pentagram** • Berlin, Germany

Seventeenth-century philosopher, John Locke, proposed that each of our senses provides input that is then translated into a singular impression. This is the basis of common sense. Pentagram partner, Justus Oehler approaches design with common sense. His attitude toward corporate communications is not based on layers of conceptual theory or oblique concepts. He asks basic questions, collects disparate pieces of information, and translates this into powerful and meaningful work. The pragmatism is apparent in the forms. The unembellished typography and imagery in other hands might be plain, but Oehler transforms these. Combined, minimal elements create a dynamic communication that is unmistakable. This, again, is purely common sense.

OPPOSITE
Serif has a simple mission, to publish books that last. Justus Oehler has designed all covers since the publisher's founding in 2002.

Each project begins with a set of questions. While Oehler may contemplate the meaning of life, or why the sky is blue, he adheres to the problem presented. "It's not so much about my philosophy, but more about the job at hand," he says, "What needs to be done? What is it that the client wants to communicate? Who does he want to reach? How much can he spend on this? Do we have text only? Do we have images? How much time do we have?" This is basic problem solving. The answers determine the most basic needs of the project. But these questions rarely lead to simple answers. Typically, clients will not answer the question, "What do you want to communicate?" with a clear answer, "Speed." Oehler distills the complex responses and multiple messages that are presented into one distinct and unique solution. To Oehler, this is the correct approach. He dismisses this ability to create order out of chaos and says, "What I need to decide is how the printed piece should look and feel in order to achieve all that it needs to achieve. Common sense, really."

The Right Thing
Doctors follow the maxim, "Do no harm." Designers follow the maxim, "Do the right thing." As creative individuals, however, designers can be swayed. We may know that a booklet is a good solution, but are tempted by the oversized poster. It is not a question of not doing the right thing,

but a question of wanting to design something because a designer loves it. Format is important. Whether a communication is held in the hands or viewed from a distance impacts our connection. Oehler's projects range from posters to catalogs, but each solution follows the needs of the communication. Oehler's response to this dilemma is clear: "There is only one way to choose a format: Do the right thing! Make sure that the solution does the job well."

We talk about the message, audience, meaning, delivery, and a multitude of other issues when designing a corporate communication. Oehler brings us back to the primary issue, "You're handed a piece of printed communication. You react to it before you even read what it says. If you dislike the look of it, you will throw it in the nearest bin. That's failed communication." Oehler creates work that is seductive. He uses forms and color that attract the viewer. He understands that human beings may not all have perfect vision and uses type that is large enough to read. And he follows the production of a project through printing. As he says bluntly, "Bad printing makes the message look cheap."

The Top 5 Rules
1. Ask yourself, "Would this printed piece appeal to me?"
2. Ask yourself, "Would it convince me?"
3. Make it elegant.
4. Make it worth keeping.
5. Work with printers you can trust!

ABOVE AND OPPOSITE There is no template that would organize the typography or imagery on the Serif book covers. Each design is tailored to the needs of the books. The designs are simple and striking, and graphic rather than photographic.

This gives the books a family look. Oehler's cover designs reinforce the client's belief that whether a book deals with cookery or civil war, foreign travel or historical theory, its design and production should be of the the of the highest quality.

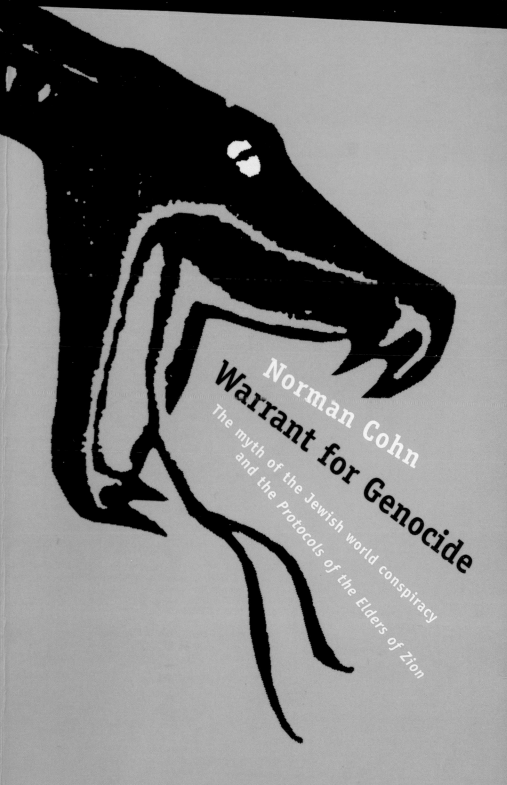

Norman Cohn

Warrant for Genocide

The myth of the Jewish world conspiracy
and the *Protocols of the Elders of Zion*

RIGHT, OPPOSITE,
AND PAGES 44–45
The DRK Hospital Group
Annual Report reflects
a sense of yin and yang,
give and take, and the fact
that there are two sides
to everything. The design
Oehler produced has the
text on the left-hand side,
faced by an illustration
on every right-hand side.
These illustrations loosely
visualize the headlines.

Kopf & Herz

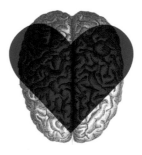

DRK Kliniken Berlin / 4. Unternehmensbericht

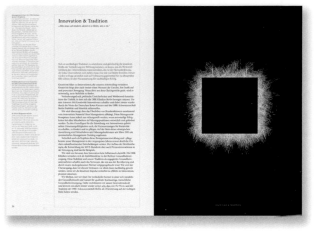

"Find a printer who is willing to help you achieve great results, and who can teach you the secrets and tricks of the trade."
—Justus Oehler

Reading Alone

Print is part of our culture. It has been a part of almost every individual's life on a daily basis for hundreds of years. One theory posits the idea that printed matter revolutionized our sense of self. Before most of the population was literate, society focused on the group. As literacy expanded, this changed. Reading forces introspection. It is an act that we do alone and in our minds make images and ideas. This act of reading leads to the importance of self. We now live in a society where the individual and the idea of individual growth is the priority. Oehler uses this visceral attachment to his advantage. He explains, "On-screen communication can do a lot, but you cannot touch it, and you cannot fold it up and carry it with you, you can not write on it." For Oehler one of the greatest benefits of printed communication is that brochures, books, and posters can be exchanged as gifts. This simple act demonstrates that printed matter represents an actual value; a website consumed online does not have any tangible value.

Oehler acknowledges the downside of printed matter and its impact on the environment. "We should consider the environment in everything we do! But all graphic designers should acknowledge that what they do is probably having a negative effect on the environment." His point here is that, as designers it is almost impossible for us to not harm the environment, but we can try to cause as little damage as possible. Oehler takes several steps to follow the most sustainable practices possible on a project. He suggests, "Do not encourage your clients to print huge quantities when they don't need them. Try and reduce the page count whenever possible. And make sure your design is beautiful—this will prevent people from throwing it away."

The Charmed Life

From afar, Oehler's work appears to have been produced with no worries. The simple and strong forms are confident and suggest the inevitable. But as with all designers, Oehler is challenged. "All parts are equally challenging," he says, "The first meeting with the client, winning the job, the design brief, the creative phase, the design presentation, producing final designs, and having stuff printed." It is the admission and understanding that all parts are challenging that is a reason for Oehler's success. It is easy to do the expected, the safe, the consistent. But each of his projects are unique and strives for excellence. The pieces take risks and he stands behind each one without fear. This is the true challenge of great work.

High-Tech Nd-YAG-Laser

Bereits 2005 konnte der neue Nd-YAG-Laser für die Thoraxchirurgie in der Chirurgischen Klinik am Standort Mitte in Betrieb genommen werden, der zweite dieser Art in Berlin. Speziell für die Lungenchirurgie entwickelt, hat er besondere Eigenschaften, die das Schneiden von Lungengewebe ermöglichen. Mit ihm ist der Thoraxchirurg in der Lage, bluttrocken und übersichtlich durch das Lungengewebe zu schneiden, wodurch Metastasen und Tumore onkologisch sicher entfernt werden können. Dadurch kann die Prognose unserer Patienten weiter verbessert werden.

Investitionen für mehr Menschlichkeit

Neben den millionenschweren Investitionen in moderne Medizintechnik ist den DRK Kliniken Berlin auch immer an der weiteren Aufwertung unserer Angebote im Sinne des verbesserten Kontaktes mit den von uns versorgten Menschen gelegen. Hierfür sprechen insbesondere die Anstrengungen, die 2007 im Zuge der Modernisierung der DRK Kliniken Berlin I Pflege & Wohnen Mariendorf unternommen wurden. Mehr Lebensqualität zu schaffen, stand hier im Zentrum unserer Anstrengungen.

Patientenorientierung

An der Klinik für Anästhesiologie, Intensivmedizin und Schmerztherapie an den DRK Kliniken Berlin I Köpenick wurde ein Kunstprojekt mit dem Ziel initiiert, die Patientenzimmer auf der Intensivstation individuell mit speziell dafür erstellten, farblich abgestimmten Bildern auszustatten, um den Patienten positive optische Reize zu bieten. Dieses Projekt ist durch eine professionelle psychologische Patientenbefragung positiv evaluiert worden.

Mensch & Maschine

„Die Maschine soll dem Menschen dienen, nicht der Mensch der Maschine."

„Menschen helfen Menschen", so lautet der Grundsatz, dem wir uns verpflichtet fühlen. Dabei bedienen wir uns moderner technischer Geräte und neuester Behandlungsmethoden. Erst wenn technologischer Fortschritt und fachliches Können mit menschlicher Zugewandtheit und offener Kommunikation kombiniert werden, wird wirksame Behandlung möglich.

Menschlichkeit ist der erste der sieben Grundsätze des Deutschen Roten Kreuzes und steht im Zentrum der Arbeit unseres Unternehmens. Moderne, vielfach hochtechnisierte Gesundheitsversorgung wird demgegenüber häufig als kalt und anonym wahrgenommen. Der Mensch, umringt von Geräten, wird scheinbar auf ein klinisches Objekt reduziert.
Die Erfolge in der medizinischen Versorgung der letzten Jahrzehnte gehen oftmals auf die Errungenschaften medizin- und verfahrenstechnischer Innovationen zurück. Ein Schwerpunkt unseres Unternehmens ist daher, dieses Potenzial auch für unsere Patienten zur Verfügung zu stellen. Kontinuierliche Investitionen in diesem Bereich helfen, unser Versprechen der bestmöglichen, sichersten und qualitativ hochwertigsten Versorgung für die Bürger dieser Stadt zu erfüllen.

Die Inbetriebnahme des Nd-YAG-Lasers 2005, Investitionen in OP-Modernisierungen und das High-end Angebot der Strahlentherapie stehen für diese Strategie. In anderen Innovationen zeigt sich deutlich auch unser Streben nach mehr Menschlichkeit in der Versorgung. So ist die Kooperation mit der Linde AG zur Heimbeatmung von Patienten 2007 zwar zunächst eine Partnerschaft zur medizinisch hochwertigen, sicheren und wirtschaftlichen Versorgung von beatmungspflichtigen Patienten. Durch dieses Angebot wird jedoch die Versorgung von Patienten mit ungenügender Atemleistung außerhalb von Intensivstationen ermöglicht. Patienten können so in den DRK Kliniken Berlin I Pflege & Wohnen Mariendorf durch moderne Beatmungsgeräte versorgt werden. Eine den sozialen und menschlichen Bedürfnissen der Betroffenen angemessenere Versorgung wird erleichtert.

Menschlichkeit ist in unserer Unternehmensentwicklung auch in einer anderen Form von großer Bedeutung. Zu jeder Entscheidung, neue Geräte oder Verfahren für unsere Arbeit einzusetzen, steht immer auch ein intensives „Change-Management". Dies beinhaltet nicht nur, die Einflüsse der Neuerung auf die krankenhausinternen Prozesse oder die Personalplanung zu analysieren. Auch der Einfluss auf den Umgang mit den Patienten spielt dabei eine bedeutende Rolle. Dieses Bemühen zeigt sich letztlich auch in der Gestaltung unserer Angebote oder der Einrichtung von Sprechstunden für die Fragen der Patienten, denn Menschen suchen vor allem in der Bedürftigkeit des Heilungsprozesses nach einer Vertrauen schaffenden Atmosphäre.
Innovation darf die Medizin nicht vom Menschen distanzieren, denn am Ende jeder noch so modernen Technologie steht das Unterstützung suchende Individuum.

26

MENSCH & MASCHINE

Bildungszentrum für Pflegeberufe plus Innerbetriebliche Fort- und Weiterbildung (IBF): Kompetenz in Pflege

■ Unser Gesellschafter, die DRK-Schwesternschaft Berlin, leistet mit seinem staatlich anerkannten Bildungszentrum einen wichtigen Beitrag zur Qualifizierung von professionell Pflegenden im Land Berlin. So werden mit 280 Ausbildungsplätzen fortlaufend junge Menschen für die Betreuung Kranker und Pflegebedürftiger herangebildet. Mit der Zusammenführung des Bildungszentrums an einem Standort (s. S. 49) können die durch das Krankenpflegegesetz 2004 gestellten neuen Anforderungen an die Lehrkräfte besser bewältigt und der Unterricht noch effektiver gestaltet werden.

■ Die praktische Ausbildung auf hohem Niveau anzubieten, war immer wichtiges Anliegen der DRK-Schwesternschaft Berlin. Unter Leitung der IBF wurden deshalb seit über 10 Jahren Mentorenkurse (heute Praxisanleiterkurse) durchgeführt. Diese dienen der geplanten kontinuierlichen Anleitung der Krankenpflegeschüler auf den Stationen und Abteilungen. Mitte 2004 wurde auf Landesebene eine neue Richtlinie verabschiedet, die inhaltlich und formal die Qualifikation der Praxisanleiter im Bereich Kranken- und Altenpflege im Land Berlin konkretisiert. Direkt im Anschluss begannen wir mit der Anpassung der Inhalte und der Planung des Programms für die Qualifizierung zum Praxisanleiter. Anfang 2005 begannen erste Kurse.

■ Im Berichtszeitraum führte die IBF verschiedene Lehrgänge durch. Die staatlich geregelte Weiterbildung „Lehrgang zur Heranbildung von Pflegefachkräften für leitende Funktionen der Pflege in Einrichtungen des Gesundheits- und Sozialwesens" absolvierten 17 Teilnehmerinnen. Die Evaluation dieser zweijährigen berufsbegleitenden Weiterbildung zeigte deutlich auf, dass die Gestaltung des Lehrgangs zur Weiterentwicklung der Handlungskompetenz in den Stations- und Funktionsbereich sehr beigetragen hat und der Lernzuwachs auch von den Teilnehmerinnen selbst als hoch eingeschätzt wurde. Der Schwerpunkt der Weiterbildung wurde im Unterricht und in den Praktika auf die Herausbildung von Fähigkeiten zur Steuerung und Optimierung komplexer Prozesse in Krankenhäusern durch leitende Pflegende gelegt. Die notwendige Verknüpfung von Management und Pflege konnte – als Novum – durch die gemeinsame Kursleitung von je einer Vertreterin des Zentralen Pflegemanagements und der IBF erfolgreich realisiert werden. Dadurch konnte beispielsweise bei Einhaltung des Rahmenlehrplans zugleich zeitnah auf die notwendig gewordenen Umstrukturierungen in unseren Kliniken reagiert werden. Nach der immer wieder notwendigen Anpassung an die aktuellsten Entwicklungen im Krankenhaus wird im Jahr 2006 ein Folgekurs eingerichtet.

■ Die Seminare „Begleitung Sterbender" wurden von 87 Pflegenden besucht. In der Auseinandersetzung mit diesem Thema wurde vor allem Sicherheit im Umgang mit Sterbenden und ihren Angehörigen vermittelt, um menschlich und professionell dem besonderen Anspruch dieser Tätigkeit gerecht zu werden. Seit 2005 ist dieses Seminar auch für andere Berufsgruppen geöffnet.

■ Zur Förderung der prozessorientierten Pflegedokumentation fanden an allen Standorten insgesamt 39 Vor-Ort-Schulungen mit 406 Teilnehmern statt. Die Erfassung der individuellen Bedürfnisse und Bedarfe der Patienten sowie die Abbildung der guten Qualität der geleisteten Pflege waren vorrangige Ziele.

■ Im 4. Quartal 2005 fanden für 31 Teilnehmerinnen zusätzlich Basisseminare zum Thema Pflegeprozess statt. Diese bilden die Grundlage für die anschließende Multiplikatorenausbildung für dieses Themengebiet.

Rund 1000 Menschen arbeiten in den DRK Kliniken Berlin und in den DRK-Schwesternschaft Berlin. Das Bildungszentrum für Pflegeberufe (s. u.) bietet noch einmal 280 Ausbildungsplätze.

BEWEGLICH

Wer bewegte Ziele ansteuert, muss in hohem Maße reaktions- und manövrierfähig sein. Es gilt, neue Anforderungen zu bewältigen, Chancen frühzeitig wahrzunehmen und Risiken zu umschiffen. Hohe Flexibilität in allen Aspekten der unternehmerischen Aktivitäten ist das Gebot der Stunde.

Das erste Medizinische Versorgungszentrum in Trägerschaft eines Krankenhauses in Berlin wurde im November 2004 an den DRK Kliniken Berlin | Mark Brandenburg eröffnet. Das Gesundheitsmodernisierungsgesetz sieht seit 2004 diese neue Form der ambulanten Versorgung vor. Die DRK Kliniken Berlin haben sich bewegt.

Der freiwillige Umstieg auf das neue DRG-Vergütungssystem mit unseren drei Krankenhäusern zum 01.01.2003 war ein mutiger Schritt. Nur vier weitere Krankenhäuser in Berlin haben den Umstieg zum Jahresbeginn 2003 vollzogen.

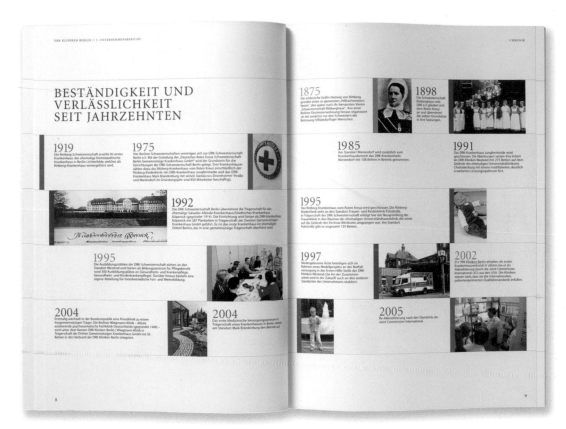

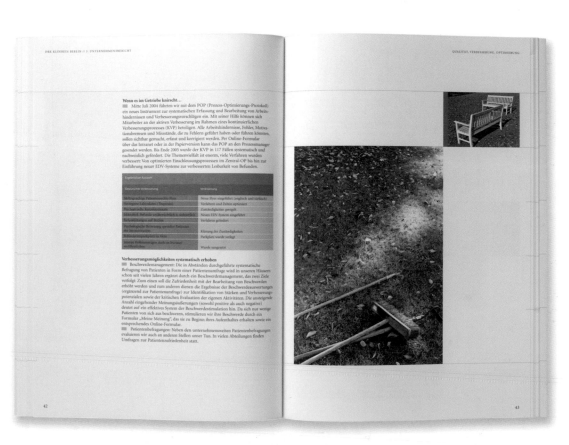

Product-

Inspired by the **1930s** military khakis.

Cut from authentic Cramerton® Army Cloth – he fabric commissioned by the Armed Forces in 1932 – how produced exclusively Dockers® Khakis by **GALEY & LORD,** mill that created it.

MERTON® ARMY CLOTH, a durable 9.0 oz. twill made with ly combed cotton yarn.

Appointed with ntic military features.

UNISEX PANT– e style, one fit – orever stay the same.

DOCKERS® **K-1** KHAKIS ADOPTED U.S. ARMY 1932
CRAMERTON® Army Cloth
FUNDAMENTALS
9.0 oz. CRAMERTON® ARMY CLOTH
CUT FROM THE ORIGINAL U.S. MILITARY MOLD
MELAMINE BUTTONS DURABLY CONSTRUCTED BROKEN-IN FEEL
WORKED OVER TO PROVIDE WIDE FLY FACING

CUT FROM THE ORIGINAL CLOTH®

Gaby Brink

Tomorrow Partners • San Francisco, California, USA ●

There is an easy trap to fall into as a designer. That trap is the prison of "cool." The partners at Tomorrow, Gaby Brink, Jeff Iorillo, and Tom Rosenfield, are masters at avoiding this trap. The work they create at Tomorrow is about human connections. "I think that esoteric, hipper-than-thou stuff doesn't cut it with real people in the real world, which happens to be where most of our clients live," explains Brink. The heavy consideration of the audience results in a relevant look and feel for a specific group. This sets off the chain reaction in the viewer's mind and heart, as Brink describes, "this transforms curiosity into belief."

OPPOSITE
Dockers set out to develop an iconic khaki, strategically in sync with the 501 in Levi's jean lineup. Dockers K-1 Khakis is aimed at a younger, trend-current audience. The authenticity of the brand is inspired by the first khakis developed for the U.S. Army in the 1930s. Working closely with Dockers' product designers, Brink built a brand that looks and behaves so authentically, one might well believe the U.S. Army created it during that era.

THE STANDARD
STRENGTH. STYLE. TRADITION.

BREAK SEAL TO ACCESS
VITAL DOCUMENTS

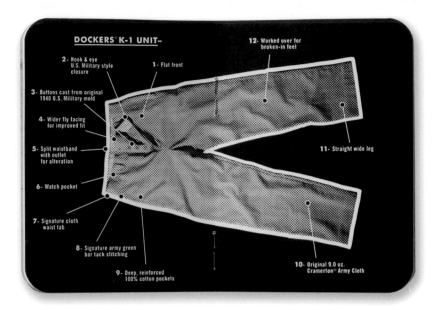

DOCKERS® K-1 UNIT-

1- Flat front

2- Hook & eye
U.S. Military style
closure

3- Buttons cast from original
1940 U.S. Military mold

4- Wider fly facing
for improved fit

5- Split waistband
with outlet
for alteration

6- Watch pocket

7- Signature cloth
waist tab

8- Signature army green
bar tack stitching

9- Deep, reinforced
100% cotton pockets

10- Original 9.0 oz.
Cramerton® Army Cloth

11- Straight wide leg

12- Worked over for
broken-in feel

The solutions at Tomorrow are successful not because they are beautifully crafted, well considered, and clear, but because they speak to a viewer intellectually and emotionally. The work is direct and idea driven with an obvious understanding of the audience.

The connection to audience and pursuit of emotional resonance are primary drivers in Tomorrow's work. These attributes permeate the conceptual and formal choices and continue into the format chosen for each communication. Brink says, "The first consideration is context. Where is our audience experiencing our client's product or service, and how can we best connect with them there?" That place can be the physical world or electronic world. She asks, "Do we have a captive audience; are we reaching out to them or are they coming to us? Are we having an intimate conversation or do we only have their attention for a fleeting moment?" The answers dictate the format from a booklet or poster, to a website or email campaign. The format is never driven by the desire to use a specific medium because the designer is more comfortable with one rather than another.

Confidence and Sustainable Options

One commonality in all of Tomorrow's work is confidence. Each solution unapologetically has a reason to be. This is a result of smart and deliberate choices. Brink explains, "If the format has an element of surprise and delight and its 'reason to be' conceptually stems from the core idea we're communicating, it's sure to be more engaging." Tomorrow's commitment to sustainable choices is also a factor in the decision of what to make and how. As an advisor to the AIGA Center for Sustainable Design, Brink promotes the integration of sustainable solutions to the design and business community. She describes her process, "I think about where a piece will go at the end of its life—how we can keep it out of the landfill for as long as possible? If it can inspire another use or life cycle, fantastic; if it can be reduced to less than you'd first expect, even better. Not only because it's more sustainable, but because brevity rules in a world where people are inundated with communication all day long."

ABOVE
The Dockers' sales force faced an uphill climb getting product into retail. Their mission was to elevate the sales channel from mass merchandise stores to specialty and fashion retailers. Proving that even a sell-in presentation can be a powerful brand-building experience, Brink created an oversized steel ammo case that had eyes popping just by walking in the room.

It contained lavish briefing documents, product blueprints, and military-style writing. This business-to-business presentation became a branded experience that opened doors, taking the brand from the pants department to the men's collections department and specialty retailers like Fred Segal and Rolo.

ABOVE AND LEFT
San Francisco's Frameline Film Festival is the world's largest celebration of lesbian, gay, bisexual, and transgendered cinema. The provocative, out-of-home campaign and comedic intheater trailer increased the festival's recognition and prestige. Past campaigns traditionally featured a single graphic icon implemented across all promotional materials. In its thirty-first iteration, Brink celebrates the diversity of the LGBT community and the colorful films it produces with a rainbow of memorable film stills.

Firm Profile

/ Asia
/ Australia
/ Europe
/ United States

"Every brand has an essential point-of-view that should be as consistent as the sun in the sky." —Gaby Brink

ABOVE AND OPPOSITE
With over 1,500 employees globally, EDAW is one of the world's leading land design firms. Project scopes range from Olympic villages to urban waterfront development. EDAW's disciplines range from design, planning, and environmental studies to economics and more. Their corporate brochure illustrates the various practices through a simple message that would appeal to its extremely diverse client base. While the solution is understated and elegant, it reflects EDAW's integrated approach with a layout structure that creates a unifying concept organizing EDAW's projects by scale rather than practice. This allowed Brink to tell the innovative stories behind their projects in a context that crossed disciplines and engaged all readers.

"Extremely important," is how Brink describes Tomorrow's attitude toward sustainable options. "Designers are makers of stuff," she continues, "therefore, we have an inherent responsibility to advise our clients to be environmentally and socially responsible." The conceptual base, the strategic direction, and brand distinctions guide Tomorrow's sustainable choices. They remain committed to helping clients align corporate strategy with environmental and social benefits. They also adhere to the basics of sustainable practices. "At times, we can only influence a client's materials consumption. For the latter, we make an effort to only use FSC-certified paper. We support mills, printers, and manufacturers that are leaders in sustainable practices," says Brink. Tomorrow does not rigidly adhere to the sustainable dogma *du jour*; they understand that sustainability is about changing behaviors, not simply changing materials. There are instances where the conversation leads to the realization that a printed piece is not needed. And, as Brink says, "that's okay."

The Story
Committing to sustainable options would suggest that Tomorrow has abandoned printed matter in favor of digital communication and websites. The reality is less black and white or blindly dogmatic. In the end, responsible sustainable choices include how an object is made and with what materials, and whether the object should exist at all. While Tomorrow works in multiple media, they maintain a commitment to print when it is appropriate. "In today's fast-paced mediascape, print communication is an invitation to slow down," Brink says. "It can bring clarity to complexity, make an emotional connection, and surprise and engage in ways that can be tactile and memorable." Printed matter, when responsibly chosen and produced, has the advantage of being linear in nature. It is a narrative, controlled by the designer, with a beginning, middle, and end. As Brink continues, "The content and the experience in print are finite."

Compostmodern 09
Convergence

Fertile ground for
sustainable design

John Bielenberg_ Project M
Allan Chochinov_ Core77
Dawn Danby_ Autodesk
Eames Demetrios_ Eames Office | Kymaerica
Pam Dorr_ HERO Housing Resource
Michel Gelobter_ Cooler
Saul Griffith_ Makani Power
Emily Pilloton_ Project H Design
Nathan Shedroff_ CCA Design MBA
Joel Makower_ GreenBiz.com, Emcee

Saturday_ February 21_ 2009
Herbst Theatre
San Francisco_ California

Tickets and webcast registration at
www.compostmodern.org

 the professional association for design

Compostmodern 09
Convergence

Fertile ground for sustainable design

John Bielenberg_ Project M
Allan Chochinov_ Core77
Dawn Danby_ Autodesk
Eames Demetrios_ Eames Office | Kymaerica
Pam Dorr_ HERO Housing Resource
Michel Gelobter_ Cooler
Saul Griffith_ Makani Power
Emily Pilloton_ Project H Design
Nathan Shedroff_ CCA Design MBA
Joel Makower_ GreenBiz.com, Emcee

Saturday_ February 21_ 2009
Herbst Theatre
San Francisco_ California

Tickets and webcast registration at
www.compostmodern.org

AIGA the professional association for design

The Top 5 Rules

1. Think about with whom you're connecting and how you can best engage them.
2. Lead with an idea and bring it to life with a relevant creative execution.
3. Design for what will resonate with your audience, not for what appeals to designers.
4. Write with clarity and brevity. Think about the problem you are solving for your audience and let it tell you what to do.
5. Think about where the material comes from, where it will go, and how it can be less.

Tomorrow's work for one of the world's leading land design firms, EDAW, exemplifies the strengths of their work. On cursory examination, the corporate brochure created is simple, strong, and confident. Upon closer examination, it is apparent that the simplicity of forms is deceiving. The solution may look simple, but the content is multilayered and strategically precise. The problem presented to Tomorrow was to produce a brochure that represented EDAW's attributes and projects. After the competitive audit, Tomorrow found that every other similar firm presented their services by practice with letter-sized brochures featuring glossy photos. Brink explains, "We realized that this organizational format prevents readers from understanding the multidisciplinary nature of EDAW's approach because it encourages selective reading." This statement is about a finding and direction, but there is a clear subtext of audience perception and how the final viewer will connect to EDAW as a whole.

The formal choices are also dictated by content and audience usage. The brochure is intimate in format and features tritone photography, a unique choice in this industry. The pages illustrate EDAW's various practices through a simple concept and message that appeals to their extremely diverse client base. Then Tomorrow takes a hard left turn from the usual. The content is organized by scale of project rather than by practice. Brink says, "This allowed us to tell the diverse stories behind EDAW's work in a context that all readers could enjoy. As a result, potential clients are engaged to learn about fascinating projects that fall outside the areas of expertise that fit their particular needs." The result of this choice is the creation of a more holistic understanding of the client's comprehensive breadth of options.

Brand and Connection

"Every brand has an essential point of view that should be as consistent as the sun in the sky," says Brink. "As designers, we have the luxury of setting the guardrails that define a brand essence." There are instances where our task is not to reinvent a brand, but to extend it by staying true to the simple truths that make it unique. Tomorrow's broad creative palette is essential to successfully tuning into those visual and editorial nuances. Listening and understanding are two of the most critical aspects of any process. Tomorrow is able to filter the information given to them by a client and connect it with audience perception and, more importantly, response. Brink explains, "My clients know more about their business than I do. I make sure that they feel like our collaborators-in-chief. This gives them ownership in the work we create together and invariably makes the process smoother and the end result more successful." It is this leap of faith, this ability to sit still and hear, that propels Tomorrow's work into successful world-class projects.

PAGES 54–55 AND ABOVE
Compostmodern is the largest interdisciplinary design conference dedicated to keeping the sustainable practice conversation fresh and relevant to the design and business communities. An abstract series of provocative designs evoke the conference theme that demonstrates how sustainable solutions converge as design, ecology, social activism, business, and economics intersect.

OPPOSITE
OracleMobile was leading Oracle's charge to wireless e-business communication. Known for its consistent corporate representation, Oracle wanted to leverage their existing brand recognition in this new category. *Tomorrow* established a clear connection with the Oracle logo using typographic elements from the company name. The branding program maintains a simple, clean style, fresh new colors, and a modern graphic architecture to distinguish the new division from its parent with unexpected vibrancy. This poster series was created to generate internal buzz for the launch of the new division.

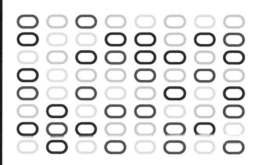

e-business

4

The Code for Success

Oracle makes it easier to compete and to make the leap from Web to wireless. OracleMobile, the mobile products and services division of Oracle, offers the company's most comprehensive set of mobile product and service offerings.

com

mobile

5

Hosting: Software as a Service

Oracle offers mobile hosting services that are professional, reliable, and secure. Oracle's professional services team has more than 60 years of combined experience, and its mobile hosting solutions are designed to meet your unique business objectives.

com

you

1

The Future of Software

According to a recent report from Morgan Stanley Dean Witter, more than 87% of CIOs are considering, or would be willing to consider having their software hosted by an ASP.

com

build

3

Solutions for Every Type of Company

Oracle's approach to mobile hosting offers distinct benefits to any company. If you're a traditional enterprise, a carrier, wireless service provider, or an Internet company and you want to give your customers, partners, or employees mobile access to information, Oracle can help.

com

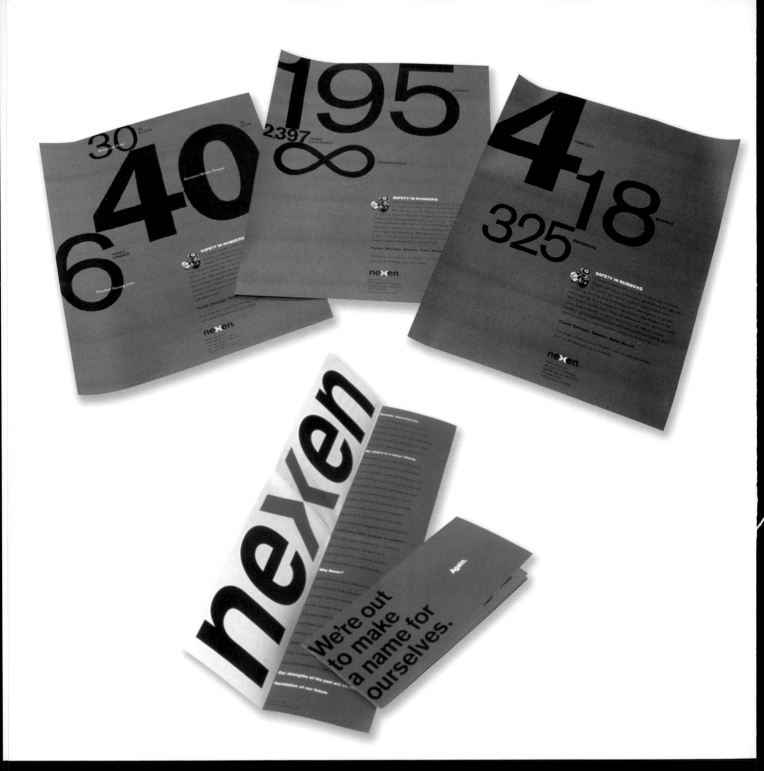

The name, *nexen*, a
six-letter palindrome, was
coined by Larsen. Nexen
Group is a manufacturer
of clutches, brakes, and
rotary motion-control
products. The name cap-

motion integral to
this manufacturer of
clutches, brakes, and
rotary motion-control
products. The brand
identity also suggests
motion and control with
its pleasing symmetrical

Print materials for a capital
campaign to upgrade the
Minneapolis Public Library
communicated the need
for increased space and

powerful personal stories.
To provide motivation and
involvement, Larsen invited
members of the community
to "Be Part of the Story."
The program helped The

THE SMART FUTURE

2007
ANNUAL REPORT

ITRON

Janet DeDonato   Dale Hart   Anne Traver

Methodologie • Seattle, Washington, USA ●

"Make the meaning unmistakable," says Janet DeDonato, a partner at Methodologie in Seattle. Along with partners Anne Traver and Dale Hart, DeDonato leads a team that is committed to creating meaningful and aesthetically beautiful materials. She is committed to the philosophy of clear communication. "Design should make a message easier to grasp. The reader shouldn't need to work too hard to get the point," she says. But this pragmatic approach and explanation does not account for Methodologie's ability to use design to do more. They create communications that shift perceptions, change behavior, and strengthen relationships. The recognition of design as a vehicle for change has driven the firm to create communications that transcend the ordinary and expected.

"The real kiss of death in a printed piece is one that has nothing important to say."

—Janet DeDonato

RIGHT
The goal of this report was to demonstrate a clear link between business strategy with progress and results. The report needed to communicate in a way that was uniquely Coca-Cola and engage readers through the same spirit and energy of the Annual Review. Readers are led to the updated website for more detailed information.

We may be best known for the shape of our bottle, but we are also passionate about shaping the world— one community at a time.

Each of us leaves a mark on the planet and on one another. At The Coca-Cola Company, we are committed to making a positive mark on communities and minimizing our impact on the planet. Together with our bottling partners and suppliers, other businesses, community leaders, governments and nongovernmental organizations, we are working to improve lives, fuel local economies and protect the environment. That is the mark we want to make.

LEFT AND PAGES 68–69
After 120 years in business The Coca-Cola Company still hasn't revealed the recipe for its signature product, but the *2006 Annual Review* spells out how the world's most recognized brand stays on top—a secret they are eager to share. Design and production involved complex project management, with photo shoots in Canada, Egypt, India, and the United States.

North America

North America is the birthplace of Coca-Cola and home to our Company headquarters. In the United States and Canada, we focus on environmental stewardship and youth development, as well as promoting active lifestyles.

Youth Development

Coca-Cola Scholars Foundation: The Coca-Cola Company and many of our bottling partners fund the Coca-Cola Scholars Foundation. The total number of students who have received support since the program's inception in 1986 reached 3,750 in 2007. To date, $32 million in educational scholarships has been awarded to college-bound high school seniors. The scholarship criteria focus on leadership, academics and service. An example of this service in action is a Coca-Cola Scholar (far left in photo) who spent two years working for Teach for America after graduating from college.

Reaching Out: Coca-Cola associates in the United States volunteer their time through our Company's "Reaching Out" program. Through this program we support many educational programs, such as tutoring elementary and middle school children. Centennial Place Elementary School located near our Company headquarters in Atlanta is one such school that receives tutors from The Coca-Cola Company.

Active Lifestyles

National Park Service: In 2007, our Company made a five-year, $2.5 million commitment to support outdoor awareness, education and recreation. Our initial commitment supports trail restoration in Yellowstone National Park and several marketing programs of the National Park Foundation.

Water Stewardship

WWF Partnership: The Coca-Cola Company and WWF have partnered to preserve and protect vital watersheds in North America, including Southeastern rivers and streams and the Rio Grande/Rio Bravo.

Energy and Climate Protection

Going Green: Our Company announced measures in 2007 to reduce energy consumption at our 2 million square foot headquarters in Atlanta, Georgia, by 23 percent and to reduce our water consumption by nearly 15 percent. These efforts are expected to eliminate more than 10,000 metric tons of carbon dioxide emissions each year, which is the equivalent of removing 2,000 cars from the road. We plan to invest approximately $3 million in energy-efficient lighting and air conditioning equipment, rainwater harvesting techniques and advanced irrigation control systems.

Sustainable Packaging

RecycleBank: We continue to expand our alliance with RecycleBank, an innovative curbside collection company. The program currently serves 20 cities throughout New England and is launching in upstate New York. RecycleBank leverages new technology and financial incentives to substantially increase household recycling participation and rates. Since its launch in 2003, RecycleBank has driven recycling rates in Philadelphia from 15 percent to more than 50 percent, and household participation from 30 percent to 90 percent.

Operating Group Statistics

Geography

Population: Approximately	Associates¹ Approximately
338 Million	12,700

Net Operating Revenues (in millions)

2004	2005	2006
$6,423	$6,676	$7,029

Operating Income (in millions)

2004	2005	2006
$1,606	$1,553	$1,683

¹As of December 31, 2006. Includes Bottling Investments.

36 The Coca-Cola Company

2006 Corporate Responsibility Review 37

Take the beverages on these two pages and multiply by 10.
Now you get a taste of our 2,600+ beverage products.

"Farmworkers have their own cultural, economic, and housing needs that require special understanding. It is due in part to the housing needs of groups like CASA of Oregon and Hacienda CDC that the housing needs of Oregon's farmworkers are being addressed. Sterling is proud to have played a small part in sponsoring this AHP application."

Kay Mooney, Sterling Savings Bank

Habitat for Humanity Maui

"The Seattle Bank's community investment programs are flexible tools that we use to help finance affordable housing. Our extensive use of both the Affordable Housing Program and the HomeStart Program allows us to support affordable rental and first-time homeownership projects and to demonstrate our commitment to our communities." Ray Mooney, Vice President / Community Development Manager, Sterling Savings Bank, Spokane, Washington

Federal Home Loan Bank of Seattle, Report of Affordable Housing and Community Investment Initiatives
2007

are the beginnings of a process leading to an appropriate message. Methodologie approaches each project with the understanding that the client will always know more about their business and their audiences than they will. They find ways to involve the client in the process. This greatly enhances the success of their projects.

Failure to Launch
It is not surprising that the characteristics of print communications that fail for DeDonato impede on the story or message. She says, "There are many ways to sabotage print communications—unclear hierarchy, a sea of gray type without subheads, competing design and typographic elements. The possibilities are endless." But the biggest culprit leading to failure is a design that obscures the message. For Methodologie, good design is about reduction and subtraction, creating order out of chaos. DeDonato continues, "But the real kiss of death in a printed piece is one that has nothing important to say."

Working with clients on large-scale projects creates a complex set of issues. As designer William Drenttel has stated, "Bigger jobs [create] bigger problems." Maintaining the integrity of a design while responding to input from multiple sources with diverse agendas is challenging. DeDonato advises, "Don't fall too much in love with your own ideas. One of the most important skills to acquire is the ability to know when to fight for an idea, and when to fold." If a client is asking a designer to do something that obscures the message, or is simply bad design that will reflect poorly on them, it is the designer's responsibility to speak up and find a solution that everyone can embrace. DeDonato admits the difficulty of this at times, "Failing that, sometimes you have to walk away," she says.

Methodologie has created a body of work that serves as a benchmark for others to meet. Their work has conveyed the client's message, and helped the client meet or exceed their business objectives. The projects are large scale and diverse, across media and format. The thinking is backed up with research, strategy, and planning. But each piece is an opportunity for an emotional connection. "I believe that eliminating touch from the experience is a big loss," DeDonato says, "The action of paging through a book and the ability to pick something up and put it down, or move around with it cannot be replicated in an online environment. People still like artifacts, and they like holding content in their hands."

OPPOSITE
Despite market turmoil in the housing industry in 2007, BRE, Inc., a California-based real estate investment trust, is confident about its future. Why? Part of the answer is "Y"—Generation Y, the seventy-plus million children of baby boomers who will flock to cities, and apartment rentals, over the next decade. With a straightforward communication style and an eye on demographics, BRE's 2007 annual report entwines the "Y" and the "Why" in a Z-fold design that gives the book two front covers. The "Y" side introduces investors to this new generation of renters and explains how BRE will work with them; the "Why" side provides a complete overview of business operations, reinforces the long-term strategy, and delivers a no-nonsense report card on the five fundamental metrics that drive business.

ABOVE
To help Microsoft connect with enterprise-level IT professionals, Methodologie partnered with Microsoft's Architecture Strategy Group to develop the Architecture Resource Center (ARC) brand and designed an identity program and a website loaded with information, research, and tools. Working within Microsoft's overall brand, the designers deliberately distilled the design of the ARC identity system and website to its essentials. The ARC website's blog, RSS feed, and webcasts open up a dialogue with the architects. Reference tools such as the printed and online *Architecture Journal* offer insights into Microsoft's vision for architecture.

Vanessa Eckstein

Blok Design • Mexico City, Condesa, Mexico ●

Like all of the best designers working with corporate communications, the work produced by Blok Design in Mexico City is clear, unique, memorable, and proprietary. But there is a duality, a contradiction in tone that succeeds in producing a product that is incredibly unique. Some designers produce work that is bold and loud. Others maintain a refined and delicate sensibility, producing projects that are coveted as beautiful artifacts. Vanessa Eckstein, principal of Blok Design, does both of these. The sparse design approach recalls a tradition of classical typography, but this subtle tone is often interrupted by large images and contrasts in color. These formal solutions do not exist purely for aesthetics; they reinforce the client's message.

OPPOSITE
El Centro, a design, film, and production design university located in Mexico City, asked Blok Design to create a simple and economical brochure to promote their university at a student event. Blok designed a poster that also doubled as an informational brochure. The materials are printed on bond paper, which gives it a contemporary feel and responds to the economic constraints. To reflect the values of a design university that believes in sustainable practices, Blok Design used all the waste produced in the print run to create envelopes with random imagery for future use in mailers.

ABOVE
Horizontes is a book designed for ING México. The book integrates a selection of landscape paintings by some of the most influential nineteenth- and twentieth-century Mexican artists from the private collection of Financial Group ING. Eckstein's typography and format reflects the Mexican landscape.

PAISAJE

lista de artistas > 13 /eduardo abaroa /francis alÿs /artemio /stefan brüggemann /verena grimm /jorge méndez blake / damián ortega /fernando ortega /rubén ortiz-torres /melanie smith /tercerunquinto /emanuel tovar /pablo vargas lugo /

sólo los personajes cambian /museo de arte contemporáneo de monterrey /el 31 de agosto de 2004 – el 13 de febrero de 2005 /monterrey /nuevo león /méxico /

"When we begin a project, we believe in listening clearly to the client's need, questioning these needs, and rethinking them," explains Eckstein. It is the ability to listen that sets Blok apart and leads to extraordinary solutions. Listening is about hearing, not judging. A client will always know his or her business better than the designer. To step into a new situation and attempt to educate a client is arrogant and will lead to conflict. Eckstein's approach of truly listening and surrendering her ego allows for more than the initial expectation on both the client and designer's sides. She says, "We always end up with a project far more interesting, unique, and functional than the one we started with." If a designer does not hear the client and presumes to already know the answer, he will invariably produce the same solution repeatedly, regardless of the client's needs. "The challenge changes from project to project, and that is what keeps us passionate and excited about each and every one of them," says Eckstein.

Intuition

Listening to the client is only the first step in Eckstein's process. "To determine the format, we need to understand who we are really speaking to and what we are trying to say," she explains. The solutions are explored using this information and maintaining communication with the client with logic and clarity. But there is a side to design that is impossible to dismiss, and Eckstein embraces that. "When all the information is clear, we rely on our intuition," she says. It is this intuition—the "messy" part of the creative process—that elevates Blok's work. Without the spark of the unexpected and personal, the work would be perfect and refined, but lack personality.

As civilization moves in one direction, there is always a longing for the past. As we move into the digital age, printed material becomes more unique and precious. Eckstein's solutions take advantage of this human response by focusing not only on the message, but also on a project's tactile characteristics. She says, "It becomes a feast for the senses and we work with the belief that it should be." Blok's work uses processes such as letterpress and embossing. The paper choice is as critical as the typography. Materials are often combined, allowing for textural changes. This produces an object that has value and makes a concrete emotional connection with the viewer.

Speaking in tongues

Multiple pieces for the same client run the risk of becoming stale and mundane. Blok sidesteps this challenge by walking the fine line of maintaining a cohesive visual language and allowing for surprise. "By understanding

ABOVE
Museo Marco's original brief was to create a catalog/book for its new exhibit on contemporary Mexican art. The book for the exhibit, *Solo los Personajes Cambia*, is a bold space for the artwork to present itself. Blok Design silkscreened the name of the different artists on the edge of the spine, questioning the existence of borders. The text is embossed on a light-sensitive material that reflects the image of the individual receiving the invitation.

LEFT AND OPPOSITE
ECO's original brief was
to create a photography
book about endangered
underwater species.
Blok chose a name that
expresses responsibility
for the environment,
and plays up the other
meaning of *echo* (trans-
lated to *eco* Spanish).
The beautiful underwater
photography was printed
with vegetable inks on
a smooth matte, 100
percent recycled stock.

FINALIDAD DE COLABORAR EN SU PRESERVACIÓN Y AGRADECERLE A LOS MEXICA
NOS SU CONFIANZA Y PREFERENCIA AL ATRAER SU ATENCIÓN Y PROMOVER LA
EDUCACIÓN CON RESPECTO A CÓMO PUEDEN CONVERTIRSE EN CONSUMIDORES
RESPONSABLES E INFORMADOS./ EN ESTA EDICIÓN SE CONCENTRA NUESTRA A
TENCIÓN EN LAS ESPECIES MARINAS, AUNQUE SON SÓLO UN EJEMPLO DE LAS RI
QUEZAS NATURALES DE LOS DIFERENTES ECOSISTEMAS EXISTENTES EN NUESTRO
PAÍS./ LA CREACIÓN DE ECO, NO HABRÍA SIDO POSIBLE SIN EL TRABAJO Y LA ES
TUPENDA LABOR REALIZADA POR EL FOTÓGRAFO MANUEL LAZCANO, QUIEN NOS
PERMITE VER A TRAVÉS DE SU LENTE PARA ENTENDER LA MAGNITUD DEL PROBLE
MA Y ADMIRAR LA BELLEZA DE NUESTRO ENTORNO./ EN NOMBRE DE ING MÉXICO
Y DEL MÍO PROPIO, CONSIDERAREMOS QUE NUESTRO PROYECTO HABRÁ SIDO EXI
TOSO SI LOGRAMOS INTERESARLOS EN EL TEMA PARA QUE HOY QUE TIENEN ESTA
OBRA EN SUS MANOS ACTÚEN Y CONTRIBUYAN CON NOSOTROS EN EL CUIDADO DE
NUESTRO ENTORNO. LA PARTICIPACIÓN DE TODOS ES NECESARIA PARA PRESERVAR
EL GRAN TESORO NATURAL DE MÉXICO./ CARLOS MURIEL, PRESIDENTE Y DIRECTOR
GENERAL DE OPERACIONES DE SEGUROS Y PENSIONES DE ING LATINOAMÉRICA.

ECO

> EN UN TRAZO RECTO LA LONGITUD DE LA LÍNEA DE COSTA MEXICANA ES EQUIVA
LENTE A LA DISTANCIA QUE VA DESDE EL NORTE DE MÉXICO HASTA EL SUR DE BRASIL.
UNAS 11 HORAS DE VUELO CONTINUO EN JET, MÁS DE UN CUARTO DE LA CIRCUNFE
RENCIA DEL PLANETA.

> EL MAR -SUS AGUAS, SUS RECURSOS PESQUEROS, SU FLORA Y SU FAUNA- A PESAR
DE LOS ABUSOS QUE HEMOS COMETIDO, BIEN MANEJADO TIENE UN GRAN POTENCIAL
DE RECUPERACIÓN. POCO TIEMPO DESPUÉS DE CUIDAR UNA ZONA MARINA, LA ABUN
DANCIA DE VIDA RETORNA. LA PESCA EN SUS ALREDEDORES SE FORTALECE, LOS PE
CES SON MAYORES.

> TODO LO QUE DESTRUYAMOS SERÁ PARA SIEMPRE, ESTAREMOS QUEMANDO LOS
PUENTES, NO HABRÁ RETORNO. EN CAMBIO TODO LO QUE CONSERVEMOS CON SALUD
AMBIENTAL DE LA ZONA COSTERA SERÁ LA BASE NATURAL PARA UNA ECONOMÍA
SANA Y SUSTENTABLE.

> EN LUGAR DE CONFRONTAR CON ENORMES DESGASTES ECONÓMICOS Y SOCIALES
AL DESARROLLO TRADICIONAL CON LA CONSERVACIÓN AMBIENTAL, DEBEMOS CREAR
A LA BREVEDAD Y DE MANERA PROACTIVA MODELOS DE DESARROLLO REGIONAL QUE
RESPONDAN A UNA VISIÓN PROFUNDA Y COMPROMETIDA.

> DE ACUERDO A DATOS OFICIALES DE LA COMISIÓN NACIONAL PARA EL CONOCI
MIENTO Y USO DE LA BIODIVERSIDAD, EL INVENTARIO CORRESPONDIENTE A LA ZONA
COSTERA Y OCEÁNICA DE MÉXICO COMPRENDE UN TOTAL DE 25,746 ESPECIES, 3,321
CATEGORÍAS INFRAESPECÍFICAS. 731 ESPECIES ENLISTADAS Y PROTEGIDAS, DE LAS
CUALES 349 SON ENDÉMICAS O ESPECIES ÚNICAS EN EL MUNDO.

> VIVIMOS UNA CONMOCIÓN, LA SIMETRÍA EN EL PODER, LA FUERZA DE LA NATURA
LEZA ANTE EL HOMBRE SE HA MANIFESTADO, NUEVOS CÓDIGOS DE DESARROLLAN,
EMPEZAMOS A COMPRENDER EL SENTIDO DEL LENGUAJE DE LOS ANIMALES, DE LOS
ECOSISTEMAS, UN NUEVO DIÁLOGO HA COMENZADO.

044

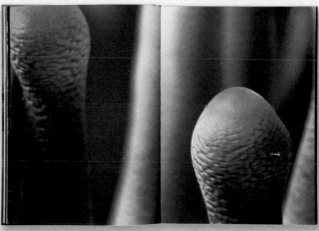

016

ECOS DE NUESTROS MARES

017

substandard product. The images in the Eco book are prominent and bold. Rather than surrendering and using less-sustainable coated paper and inks, Eckstein maintained her focus and applied curve corrections at the printing stage to maintain quality.

Eckstein says, "Working sustainably is about thinking differently about the project." The Nienkämper brochure Blok designed created one piece with many functions. It is a corporate brochure, a product specifier, and set of promotional postcards. Another example is the Centro project. The solution functions both as brochure and poster, and the printing press make-ready sheets were converted into memorable envelopes for future mailings.

Eckstein believes that design can better everyday life and remind us of our own humanity. It is this idealistic approach that pushes Blok to take risks, to never settle, to explore, and to enjoy every aspect of the project. This is not a desire to only play and create work for a small audience. There is a rigor in all pieces. And the duality of finesse and strength embodies both the optimistic approach and the passion. In a recent interview, Eckstein was asked if she were a color, what color would she be? "The word *blanco*, meaning white in Spanish," she responded, but then added, "and the word *black*. In English, this comes from the same linguistic root."

Curves

Curves is a technical term used by printers that adjust an image for printing. The curves must be adjusted for dot gain when printing on a recycled, uncoated paper. This will correct the dot size and allow the pressman to run proper ink densities that will lead to images that are saturated and have better detail.

ABOVE AND OPPOSITE
Some historians point to El Zanjon de Granados as the site of the first settlement of Buenos Aires in 1536. After sixteen years of detailed planning and renovations, the derelict mansion was restored with a clear objective of preserving the memory. Blok Design created an identity as complex and as reflective of the many historical layers as the building itself.

Through its movement and diversity, the typography conveys the essence of historical Buenos Aires ephemera. (Buenos Ayres with a *Y* as it was found written in 1700s). Blok Design built a vocabulary that encompasses pattern designs inspired by tiles from the 1860s, old city maps from different years, original illustrations, and photos of the building at various stages of development.

SAMATAMASON, INC.
WEST DUNDEE, ILLINOIS, USA

LEFT TO RIGHT
Dave Mason
Kevin Krueger

effective

Formed in 1995, SamataMason, Inc. is an acknowledged expert
in corporate communications, branding, marketing, and image
management. SamataMason works in all forms of media including
print, interactive, environments and signage, film, and video,
for clients ranging from start-ups and not-for-profits to members
of the Fortune 500. They follow a basic philosophy: do good work
for good people, and have fun doing it.

ABOVE AND OPPOSITE
TIR is a solid-state lighting
product provider for architectural, entertainment,
transportation, and special
purpose applications.
The integrated marketing
communications program
has helped TIR convey

the incredible economic,
environmental, and logisti-
cal benefits of its products
to both customers and
shareholders.

Not Your Father's **Mailroom**

Business lore is filled with stories of business executives who started in the mailroom and climbed to the chief executive office. So it's with some pride that we point out that the success of many CEOs today depends partly on the expanded and technologically sophisticated mail and document production centers they left behind – and partly on the future we bring them. Software from Bell & Howell Mail and Messaging Technologies is working to turn high-volume mailers and bulters into personal messengers. • The marketing wizards in Bell & Howell's e-Route™ software personalize a recipient's direct mail based on ZIP codes, buying preferences, income, age and other characteristics. And Bell & Howell's TransFormer™ software helps produce more readable,

easier-to-understand bills, dramatically reducing queries to call centers. These are among the Bell & Howell software solutions that enable production mailing centers – where Bell & Howell has long been the leader in inserting systems – to evolve into operations now known as "automated document factories." • But it doesn't stop there. Bell & Howell's e-Route™ Internet option is making Internet billing a reality. And while Internet billing represents only 2 percent of business-to-home mail today, it is expected to grow significantly during the next five years. Bell & Howell already has the first-mover advantage that helps take its customers straight to the top.

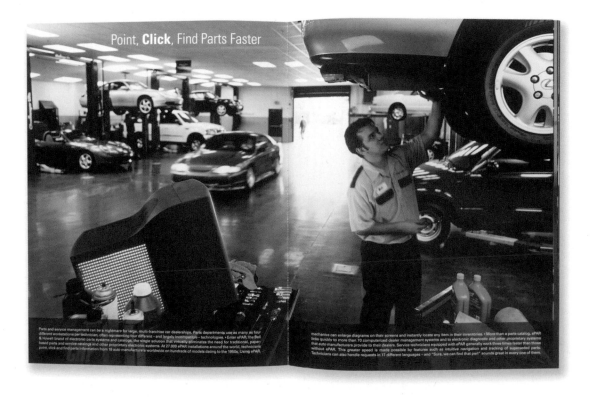

Point, **Click**, Find Parts Faster

Parts and service management can be a nightmare for large, multi-franchise car dealerships. Parts departments use as many as four different workstations per technician, often representing four different – and largely incompatible – technologies. • Enter ePAR, the Bell & Howell brand of electronic parts systems and catalogs, the single solution that virtually eliminates the need for traditional, paper-based parts and service catalogs and other proprietary electronic systems. At 27,000 ePAR installations around the world, technicians point, click and find parts information from 16 auto manufacturers worldwide on hundreds of models dating to the 1950s. Using ePAR,

mechanics can enlarge diagrams on their screens and instantly locate any item in their inventories. • More than a parts catalog, ePAR links quickly to more than 70 computerized dealer management systems and to electronic diagnostic and other proprietary systems that auto manufacturers provide to their dealers. Service technicians equipped with ePAR generally work three times faster than those without ePAR. This greater speed is made possible by features such as intuitive navigation and tracking of superseded parts. Technicians can also handle requests in 17 different languages – and "Sure, we can find that part" sounds great in every one of them.

Joseph and Nancy Essex

Essex Two • Chicago, Illinois, USA

Brand communication is at the heart of Essex Two's
philosophy. For principals Nancy and Joseph Essex,
a brand is not just a company's name or trademark—
it is its reputation. Through shared experiences with its
audiences over time, a critical relationship is established.
Values are identified, affirmed, and consistently applied
with each communication. Like most successful relationships, a client's brand requires a long-term commitment
with the understanding that change, in one form or
another, is inevitable.

OPPOSITE
While Bell + Howell is
remembered for its motion
picture projectors days,
the company has continu-
ously transformed itself for
close to 100 years. It is
currently an international
software company that

specializes in products
and services for businesses.
Essex designed the Bell
+ Howell annual report
to highlight this evolution
and transformation.

RIGHT AND BELOW
This Bell + Howell
annual report focuses on
customers and markets
across internal divisions
and brands. Essex Two
created a red monitor to
serve as an iconic device

demonstrating the
pervasiveness of Bell +
Howell products in
everyday life and to
link their many diverse
products, services,
and business groups
from around the world.

BELL & HOWELL ANNUAL REPORT 1999

No **Time** for Downtime

Long the leader in maintaining mail center finishing equipment, Bell & Howell Mail and Messaging Technologies is rapidly expanding its capabilities to enable mail and document production centers to provide "24/7" operation – without downtime. The company has buttressed its solid base of electromechanical skills with computer hardware and software specialists, programmers, trainers and network engineers to provide complete customer services. • In addition, Bell & Howell plans to acquire other service businesses and reach agreements with other manufacturers of mail and document production equipment who will profit from outsourcing their

When **Image** is Everything

Even in today's electronic age, many businesses continue to handle huge numbers of documents – checks, forms, waybills, etc. They just convert the contents of their documents into digital images suitable for instant storage, access and retrieval. And those companies are never more conscious of their image than when a mission-critical imaging system malfunctions. • Enter Bell & Howell. With its technical expertise and its 1999 acquisition of the Field Services Group of TAB Products, a leading digital maintenance service company, Bell & Howell provides technicians at 145 locations across the U.S. to maintain storage devices,

servers, scanners and other imaging components on a 24/7, four-hour response time • But it's more than just response. Bell & Howell partners with end users, value-added resellers, distributors and manufacturers to train and certify all Bell & Howell technicians in a variety of imaging components and systems. Bell & Howell service technicians also receive training in industry service programs such as CompTIA's A+ Certification for computer repair. • Should come as no surprise then, that Bell & Howell is earning the service reputation as the one number to call when image is on the line.

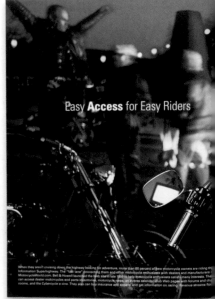

Easy **Access** for Easy Riders

When they aren't cruising down the highway looking for adventure, more than 80 percent of new motorcycle owners are riding the Information Superhighway. The "fast lane" connecting them and other motorcycle enthusiasts with dealers and manufacturers is MotorcycleWorld.com. Bell & Howell launched the Web site in late 1999 to help motorcycle enthusiasts satisfy many interests. They can access dealer motorcycles and parts inventories, motorcycle news, an events calendar, club Web pages with forums and chat rooms, and the Cybercycle e-zine. They also can buy insurance and apparel and get information on racing. Revenue streams for

Smarter Study Date

On many college campuses today, the most popular study date isn't that good-looking "A" student from across the aisle. It's ProQuest, the powerful, easy-to-use online reference source and periodical database from Bell & Howell. • Introduced in 1996, ProQuest already reaches almost two-thirds of the 15 million college students in the United States and is available in academic college libraries in more than 100 other countries around the world. Because the service so elegantly meets the needs of researchers and librarians for full texts and images, it attracts nearly 2 million page views per day. • ProQuest offers 60-70 percent full-text

availability – a direct result of the confidence publishers have that Bell & Howell will protect their interests. Its ease-of-use comes from creation of powerful indexes and sophisticated technology that steer even novices into doing the right thing to get relevant results. • Oh, one other reason ProQuest is so popular with students and researchers in libraries and dorms worldwide: It never cares what you look like.

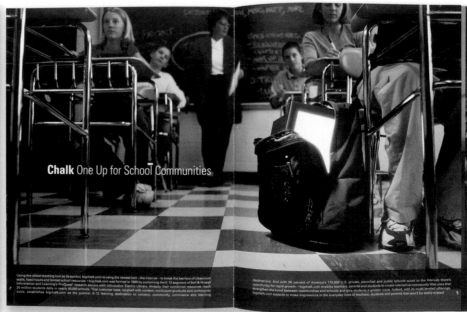

Chalk One Up for School Communities

Using the oldest teaching tool as its symbol, bigchalk.com is using the newest tool – the Internet – to break the barriers of classroom walls, fixed hours and limited school resources. • bigchalk.com was formed in 1999 by combining the K-12 segment of Bell & Howell Information and Learning's ProQuest® research service with Infonautics' Electric Library. Already, their combined resources reach 25 million students daily in nearly 40,000 schools. That customer base, coupled with content, curriculum products and community tools, establishes bigchalk.com as the premier K-12 learning destination to content, community, commerce and learning

destinations. And with 90 percent of America's 110,000 U.S. private, parochial and public schools wired to the Internet, there's opportunity for rapid growth. • bigchalk.com enables teachers, parents and students to create interactive community Web sites that strengthen the bond between communities and schools and give students a greater voice. Indeed, with its multi-leveled offerings, bigchalk.com expects to make impressions in the everyday lives of teachers, students and parents that won't be easily erased.

The "Love of Books" paper promotion for Consolidated was designed to remind designers, writers, printers, and paper specifiers of all kinds why they love the printed page. By presenting the personal stories of acknowledged peers about the books that changed their lives, readers are both drawn to the examples and asking themselves the same questions. Along with the stories were the actual books themselves as well as photographs of the designer reading the books. The best testimony for the success of this promotion is that Consolidated sold a great deal of paper.

Joseph explains, "We translate business objectives into emotional understanding. We prepare language and images that promote communication, attracting the empathy of specific audiences. Our process is not about visual manipulation or decoration, but one of discovery and clarification."

The vehicles to deliver the brand message vary depending on many factors. Essex works with the client to understand issues such as audience, budget, context, competition, and sustainability. Most large clients have been given 200-page documents that explain and document research and findings. Many of these, however, stop at this point. Essex Two handles this expectation differently. They quickly focus on the clear and direct issues, and they provide concrete direction for implementation. They ask three simple questions: *What do you want to happen? To whom do you want it to happen? What results do you expect?* The answers to these questions form criteria that lead to all communication recommendations. On the surface, these are simple, straightforward questions; however, a detailed exploration of the answers can be quite complex and very telling. Nancy says, "Our objective is not just understanding but enlightenment. When we know the reasons behind the answers, we can create communication tools that serve needs as well as wants."

Tools

A common theme shared by great designers is the acknowledgement that they will never know a client's business better than the client. Unfortunately, there are clients not experienced at working with designers. To better facilitate the process, Essex Two developed a suite of tools and services to stimulate the enthusiastic participation of the clients at every stage of the communication process. One of these tools is a simple concept employed by Essex Two at the onset of a project. This concept is the ability to assess, advise, and recommend a solution for a project, and then prepare, package, and present those recommendations to audiences in ways that promote understanding, appreciation, and participation. According to Joseph, "Services without service are just good intentions without commitment."

There is a component to design that is often overlooked: It is the public aspect that drives much of a designer's choices. As opposed to fine art, a designer creates work that will be seen by thousands or millions of people. This fact can be daunting. At Essex Two, this is used as an advantage. Joseph explains, "We never think about creating a printed communication product for 5,000 or 55,000 or 500,000 readers. We create each vehicle for one person, the person who holds it in their hands at arm's length and tries to make a connection with our client's message." The process of creating while considering

The Amazing Spider-man, July 1964
Non-Pareil Publishing Corporation

"This was the first comic book that I read and for me it was an early introduction to the literary and artistic world. This set off on or seven years of collecting comics, mainly Marvel. I have all the Spider-man issues.

"It was pure escapism for me. It may seem strange, but even at that age I felt the need for escapism. The whole idea of going into another world was one that fascinated me. I read them over and over again to myself. For me, it was a fantasy world in many ways they stay. Like a lot of kids, I had the fantasy of wanting to be a superhero, but just as much for me was the desire to be an artist for one of these magazines. I was already drawing a lot at that age, and I remember being so impressed with the drawing ability of these artists.

"But what really captivated me was the writing—it's marvelous, very clever, witty and articulate. I absorbed a lot of what I know from this medium."

The Double Helix
by James D. Watson
McClelland & Stewart Ltd., 1968

Wuthering Heights
by Emily Brontë
Random House Publishers, 1943

A Little Cowboy's Christmas
by Marcia Martin
Wonder Books,
Grosset & Dunlap, Inc. 1951

Vanity Fair, June 1983
Condé Nast Publications Inc.

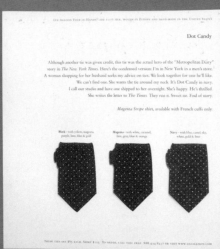

"Be honest, even when there is no reason to be honest."
—Joseph Essex

the response of one individual—as opposed to millions of faceless figures—gives Essex Two's work a personal touch. The result is work that is clear, aesthetically sophisticated and accessible, but warm and emotive.

Most clients are good at what they do but are not as good at expressing what they do how they do it, or why their customers should care. Isolation, not ignorance nor arrogance, is typically the reason for this. Every client knows their past, where they came from, and how they got here. Internally they use words, phrases, and idioms that express themselves to each other quickly and succinctly. Joseph says, "That shorthand language keeps everybody else out. To be of any real value to our clients, we need to entice them into telling the stories that made them who they are using words that don't require a trade dictionary." It is this plainspoken approach that embodies much of Essex Two's work. There is a clarity and simplicity that is more about pragmatism than decoration.

Accidental Viewing
Corporate communications take many forms. Each designer is challenged by a different format. For Essex, the easiest print piece to understand and the most difficult to produce is a poster at any size. "Booklets, brochures, and reports are destination pieces—they are usually sent for, expected, or selected by the

reader," says Joseph. "A poster is an accident. The reader discovers the poster accidentally out of the corner of an eye, from the back window of a bus or while waiting for that bus." He believes a poster must stop the viewer from 25 feet (7.6 m) away or more. If it doesn't do that, it fails. If it's not designed well enough to bring the reader closer, to see and read the larger typography and/or more fully appreciate the imagery, it again fails. If the poster overcomes these challenges and the reader has absorbed enough content to feel or act in response to the poster's message, it succeeds. Essex says, "Otherwise, it's just so much visual noise. No matter how cool it looks or the design awards it may receive, if there is no meaning for the reader, there is no success for the client or the designer."

A piece fails when there is too much content without context. This is similar to having unlimited credit in a country that only accepts its own currency. A hallmark of an Essex Two piece is the ability to manage content in bite-size pieces. Content is provided at a pace that prompts awareness and the internal dialogue of the reader, that promotes understanding and acceptance. Too much content presented in an unsympathetic or cavalier manner expresses arrogance or indifference and will not turn readers into customers.

ABOVE AND OPPOSITE The Lee Allison Company makes elegant, beautiful, rich, and fun handmade neck ties. In an effort to stimulate direct sales on the company's website, a catalog program was initiated and then expanded. The objective was to introduce a new product line of shirts and combine it with ties. Identifying lifestyle moments and capturing them photographically told a story about the shirt, the tie, and the man.

Urban Shopping Centers, Inc. Annual Report 1998

Political Identity

Cohesive message and content is important to all Essex Two endeavors. "Each component of a communication program needs to be like the Kennedy family. While each device has a different job to do, goal to accomplish, and/or information to be delivered, they all have something in common: the teeth." Individual politics aside, the Kennedy family also represents a cohesive identity perpetuated by action, not only visual connection. There is a commonality in action that contributes to a clear voice. "Constancy is more than repetition; it is about tone, temperament, attitude, and character. Things belong together because they complement each other. They add and they contribute to a collective impression. If done well, the impression is positive, even if you don't buy the product or the politics," says Joseph.

Trade Secrets

Growing a strong creative team is an ongoing and challenging task for all designers. Essex two places a high priority on the team building and mentoring of individuals. Essex doesn't simply hope that a project will succeed. Both principals impart their knowledge and expertise without reservation. This generosity of spirit extends to the firm's public communications also. They freely share information other designers may consider trade secrets. They understand that as part of a larger community, each piece of practical knowledge shared makes the profession stronger.

When advising younger designers or students, Joseph is as plainspoken as his work, "Think of each print project as a two-stage relay race. The first stage of the project is creating a brochure that does what you said it would. You compromise when you have to and stay strong when you can. You then move from design and implementation to print and production. You and your client still will fail if the ink on paper is a failure." He continues, "Support the printing process and your printer. Be honest even when there is no reason to be honest. However, don't forget you are responsible for the entire job not just the design. Lead and delegate, ask those who are supporting your efforts to do what they said they would do, and not just for this job but the next one and the next one."

ABOVE LEFT AND OPPOSITE Urban develops and manages some of the country's premier shopping centers and malls. The messages presented in this report focus on Urban's central business tenet: retail and real estate are driven by consumer perceptions of quality, and customer satisfaction takes place at every level. Essex Two designed the annual report communicating the client's achievements and goals that led to the acquisition of Urban Shopping Centers by a larger developer.

Urban Shopping Centers practices a "hands on" approach to asset management. Senior management continuously reviews the performance of each owned property on a tenant-by-tenant basis. This allows management to understand all issues relating to each property.

Asset Management

Dennis M. Zaslavsky is an Executive Vice President and the Chief Operating Officer of Urban Shopping Centers, Inc. Mr. Zaslavsky directly oversees Urban Shopping Centers, Inc.'s portfolio of properties. Prior to his joining Urban, Mr. Zaslavsky was a Senior Vice President of JMB Realty, which he joined in 1992.

Urban Shopping Centers is very focused on the asset management of its portfolio. Can you explain your general strategy for asset management? **Dennis Zaslavsky:** We believe thoroughness and attention to detail are critical to our business. As such, we visit our properties every 4-6 weeks. We have an all-day meeting attended by our CEO, CFO, COO and the heads of our management, leasing, development and marketing groups. At these meetings, we closely monitor what is occurring, space by space, at each of our properties to be sure we're doing everything necessary to have the best tenants and most productive assets possible. What makes Urban's approach unique? Our top management visits our properties on a regular basis. We emphasize a hands-on approach and recognize the need to have a complete understanding of each of our assets. We have a very cooperative process and are known to have some of the best people in the regional mall business. Many people have input as we formulate and execute our strategies. What are some examples of recent change that happened because of your in-depth review of Urban's portfolio? Penn Square Mall in Oklahoma City is a good example. We had a major lease expiration year there during 1998. Our leasing group downsized some less productive tenants, expanded more successful tenants and brought new tenants into Oklahoma City. We were able to significantly increase the productivity of our tenants and our revenue from the center because of the changes we implemented. Another recent example is Old Orchard Center in suburban Chicago. At Old Orchard, we moved Eddie Bauer into an expanded space, brought in their home furnishings concept and greatly enhanced the occupancy of our newly developed wing of the center. Does your management of so many urban properties pose any special asset management challenges? Our presence in many mixed-use downtown projects including Copley Place in Boston, Water Tower Place in Chicago and San Francisco Shopping Centre requires us to become experts with a number of unique assets. We have to understand the office and hotel issues of mixed-use properties and the challenges of urban parking. We must be familiar with the particular challenges of vertical retailing and the role tourism markets can play in our urban properties. In connection with your asset management role, you work on acquisitions. Who else at Urban participates in acquisitions? We do not have specific acquisition personnel. The professionals who will manage, lease, develop and market the property upon completion of an acquisition are the same people who participate in the acquisition process. We believe this makes for better acquisitions and also ensures better performance once we are operating the property.

Urban Shopping Centers has established strong leasing relationships with many of the country's best known retailers. With specialty retail stores, unique restaurants, and entertainment concepts, Urban is able to make their properties "destinations," not merely shopping malls.

Leasing

Ross R. Glickman is President of Leasing for Urban Retail Properties Co. From 1991 to 1995, Mr. Glickman served as an Executive Vice President of Leasing for Urban Retail Properties Company.

Leasing has been one of Urban Shopping Centers' consistent strengths as a publicly-traded REIT. What are your criteria when leasing space for an Urban property? **Ross Glickman:** We realize we must understand the demographics of each center. This translates into understanding the needs of the consumers who visit the properties. Our leasing strategies also require us to introduce new concepts into our markets, offer the only location of certain retailers in a market and expand successful tenants from one part of the country to another. It is really a question of creating a merchandise mix that caters to the demographic profile of the market, but remains fresh and exciting. How does Urban's approach to leasing differ from your competitors? We differentiate ourselves in a number of ways. First, the high quality of our properties is very appealing to retailers. Our centers are very productive with sales per square foot of $377 and occupancy of approximately 93.3%. Second, we have established a strong reputation because of the successful lease-up of our three most recent developments. We have shown that we understand our markets as well as the retailers' needs, concerns and goals. With each new success, national retailers trust our judgment more and understand that we're trying to put them in a position where they can be productive. It boils down to the relationship we have with our counterparts on the retailing side and the credibility we have developed in the owner and operator of so many successful properties. Is each Urban property separate in terms of the retail niche you are trying to create or is there a good generic mix you like to have at every property? There is a mix relative to categories that you like to accomplish, such as home furnishings, apparel or jewelry. We do not have a set formula that dissects a property's space into exact percentages by category. We work to understand the market's needs and determine who are the best retailers for that market. You also have responsibility for Urban's Marketing Department. What functions do they perform? Our marketing professionals and leasing professionals work closely together to create the proper environment for our properties. The marketing department acts as a marketing agency for each property, directing marketing programs and incorporating exclusive programming and alliances where appropriate. The department directs advertising agencies, holiday decor design, customer service, public relations and tourism. They create programming tailored to the tenant mix and designed to maximize traffic and sales, increase the customer base and maximize the frequency of visits and length of time shoppers spend at the property.

TANK CREATIVE INTELLIGENCE
PORT MELBOURNE, VICTORIA, AUSTRALIA

BABYBOOMERS THE LOVE GENERATION
SPUTNIK GENERATION
SANDWICH GENERATION

ADSHEL

INSIGHT INNOVATION AUDIENCE DELIVERY

THE FINDINGS
10 CREATIVE COMMAND

05 09
06 1
07
08

10 THINGS TO KNOW
ABOUT ADSHEL

Tank Creative Intelligence strives to create a remarkable experience. The firm has an environment that fosters a spirit where ideas thrive, individuals are respected, and smart strategy lives with innovative design. Their work cuts through the noise and makes a lasting impression. This is achieved by creating experiences that are honest, sincere, and true. They take the work seriously, but they don't take themselves too seriously.

IMPACT

ANNUAL REVIEW 08

Connell Wagner

CONVEYING BENEFITS
Abbot Point Coal Terminal

Hugh McKay, Principal, Marine

The contribution of Connell Wagner
in turning a tract of land that was
the site of an ambitious sustainable

...in our rejuvenation is to
world. Contribute through
...cial responsibility; through
...mic infrastructure; through
...wledge.

Hobsonville represents the first
Comprehensive Development Plan (CDP)
application to be completed in New
Zealand. Commissioned by Hobsonville
Land Company, a subsidiary of Housing
New Zealand Corporation, and lodged
with Waitakere City Council, the submission
outlines new benchmarks for sustainable
urban development in the coastal

Connell Wagner Auckland, as part of a
civil and environmental engineering
geotechnical consultants, worked closely
with urban designers and landscape
architects Isthmus to realise the
application for the client within
timeframes. Weekend and after hours work
wasn't uncommon for our team members.
In a true team effort, our dedicated number...

Melbourne Cares

As a founding member of Melbourne
Cares, an organisation focused on
addressing the needs of the
disadvantaged, Connell Wagner...
developed a number...

World Youth Day

Bruce Laker is passionate about
engineering career. He is equally
passionate about supporting the you...
today to inspire them to create a pos...
and vibrant future. His increasing in...
Youth Day (WYD) is indicative of...

WYD is the largest youth event in the
world, which was held in Sydney from
15-20 July 2008. Organised by the
Catholic Church, WYD brings young
people t...

LEFT
Economics Days is a
five-day event organized
by Galatasaray University
(GSU). 2 Fresh relied on
monetary symbols to
communicate the program.
Bizer used posters to
create on-campus
communications, as well
as other formats, such as
invitations, letters, an
event schedule, and a
program for academic and
bureaucratic attendees.

to a digital device. And the web requires one more step—a digital connection. Bizer considers the comfort and flexibility of pen and paper that print offers. "I believe print is a well-developed tool of humanity. Paper signifies thousands year of knowledge in its development, since the hieroglyphs of ancient Egypt."

"Design is the purposeful process of creating functional relationships. It might be between shapes, forms, words, materials, and sounds. It might be between a client and the audience. A designer should have the ability to combine things and create new relationships," says Bizer. This requires the ability to process intellectually. In today's fast-paced world, designers are expected to think, design, and produce quickly. This necessitates a designer to sharpen his or her mind and skills. "Contributions to art shows, exhibitions, or theme books and magazines are great opportunities to create. I make most of these opportunities—I experiment with new forms, new styles; I exercise on finding ideas or creating concepts. Because I know that practice makes better design, I experiment. Practice can't guarantee success, but without it, failure is inevitable," he explains.

Emotional Response

Bizer understands that people buy things they like. Once they like a product, idea, brand, they will find a reason to justify their decision, regardless of the logic. As a communications designer, Bizer creates the emotional tie and gives the audience reasons to help them justify their decision. For example, nobody makes a decision by listening to the story of a logo design or the designer's point of view. People just like it or they don't like it. If a client does like the logo, the hard work is done. If they don't, the rationale and logic won't matter. Whether the communication is liked must be determined by the audience. Bizer clarifies, "This determination must not be made by the designer, marketing team, or CEO. Only the target group in mind is important. That's where the designer should avoid clichés or mistakenly think the audience is a vast undifferentiated group. Indeed, they are not. They are individuals, they are all different human beings. This is where observation and socialization make a better designer."

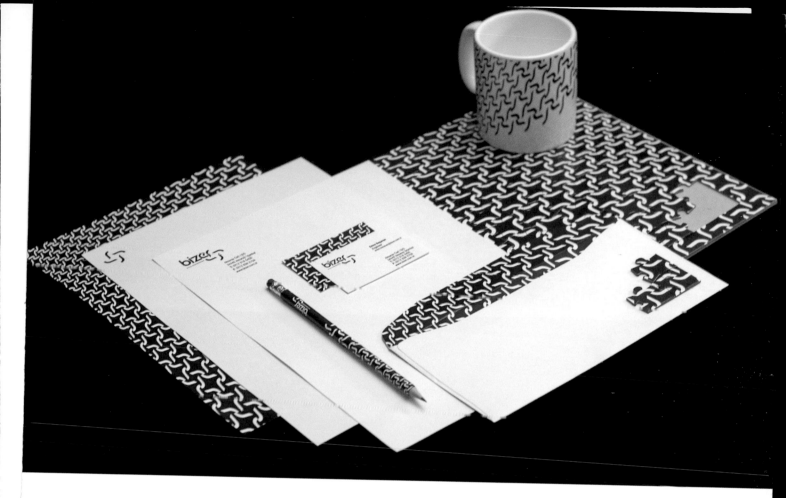

LEFT
Bizer chose to stay away from trends and visual tricks when designing the 2 Fresh identity and communications materials. He created a program that is clean, clear, timeless, and modern. Red and orange together reflect 2 Fresh's dynamism, ambition, optimism, energy, young blood, and freshness.

ABOVE
Bizer's design of HVAC items creates a seamless and integrated communication over all media. The result is a strong and effective communication in all media.

SPRING TIME IS DUTY FREE TIME

✈ ISTANBUL | ANKARA | IZMIR | TBILISI | BATUMI   🌐 atu.com.tr

atu
DUTY FREE

The Top 5 Rules
1. I don't have rules.

ABOVE AND OPPOSITE
Print communication
materials for ATU's
spring campaign refer to
the traditions of Ottoman
calligraphy. Historically,
mundane items as tax
reports, property deeds,
and imperial edicts

became exquisite works
of art. Each of the sultans
had their own monogram
in stylized script, called
a Tugra. Bizer uses these
forms in a fresh way and
transforms calligraphy
into images.

The medicines we take to grow old. / The food we eat to stay healthy.

Aagaard, Lisi / Affholter, Ise / Alton, Rigris / Abriedo, Jose / Ang, Oll / Andersen, Kim Vilbour / Apt, Doris / Åberg, Per / Aswath, Minni / Bailey, Barbara / Belatskaya, Svetlana / Bao, Steven / Beard, Clayton / Beard, Katja / Bedbrook, John / Bergman, Paul / Bermudee, Ericka / Bertain, Sean / Beyar, Nurten / Bhakta, Amit / Black, Marcella / Boosen, Thomas / Bornen, Claus / Boyce, Adam / Brenbal, Kim Seidel / Brinkmann, Alice / Briscoe, Lawrence / Burd, Parris / Carle Uriosto, Jose / Caro, Brian / Castle, Linda / Cerf, David / Chang, Jean / Christiansen, Jesper / Chatterjee, Ranjini / Chen, Bing-Yuan > 108

Chen, Michelle / Chen, Teddy / Chen, Yong Hong / Chen, Yan / Cho, Hyeon-Je / Choudhury, Patricia / Chrisman, Linda / Christini, Amanda / Clarkson, Martin / Cohen, Anh / Cong, Ruth / Cox, Anthony / Cu Unjieng, Anna / Darré, Tina / Daum, Nina / David, Nicasio / Davidsen, Kasper Danneler / Davis, Christopher / Dawes, Glenn / DelCardayre, Steve / Dhawan, Ish / Dojka, Michael / Drastrup, Jørn / Dunn, Diane / Dunne, Kathleen / Emig, Robin / English, James / Exberger, Mark / Fitzpatrick, Jules / Flyvholm, Morten / Freeman, Michael / Frederikscn, Dorte / Festgaard, Per Ola > 109

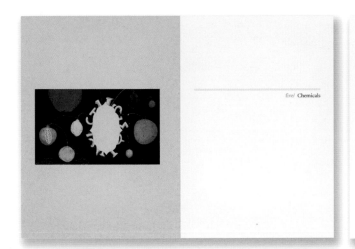

five/ Chemicals

years	months
high	low
yes	no
low	high

This alone can lead to remarkable solutions, but to reach the next step, he adds, "Typically we start any project with a deep dive into our clients' businesses and problems. We have a tendency to ask offbeat questions that cause angst. We often make our clients uncomfortable. Sometimes, we ask questions that are so obvious it can cause conflict. As a result, we not only listen to their responses, we read body language as well. We're looking to see what makes them comfortable or not."

Cahan maintains reaching this goal has as much to do with the client as the designer. "Typically, the most challenging part of a project is the client. We're only as good as the people who hire us," he says. This often requires working directly with the person in the C-suite [the CEO]. Work that is informed from the top down of the organization is more effective. This connection with final decision makers ensures that middlemen are not diluting the message and that the finished solution will be supported and endorsed at the top. "It takes a client willing to stand up for the solution, and defend it, to make great design," explains Cahan.

Respect

Conversely, design that doesn't succeed has common factors: clients who micromanage, work driven by fear of failure, and management by a large group. Great design isn't necessarily something that everyone in an organization agrees with. In fact, if everyone agrees, there's probably something wrong with the design. "Graphic design is great when it causes a reaction. Indifference is the kiss of death," Cahan notes. Also, a great client sees the designer as a partner, and treats them as such. It's "commensurable"—when the designer and client support each other and look at each other as teammates. Cahan explains that this is a simple thing that clients should understand. "When they treat us with respect, we give them better service. We work harder for them. In fact, we'll do anything for them!"

Cahan has had to redefine corporate communications over the twenty-three years his firm has been in business. "It certainly isn't what it was in the past. It used to mean something specific, mostly printed things, but now it's all branding," he says. Today, corporate communications take many forms and formats. But Cahan believes it's still about telling clients' stories in compelling ways, regardless

of the final choice of media. "Really effective communication design is all about thinking. Great thinking can be applied to any delivery medium. How can you tell a great story? And how can you make that story compelling? That's the heart of it." He adds, "Sometimes, however, I feel like a twenty-three-year-old start-up company."

Brand

Each project at Cahan & Associates is tackled with a larger picture in mind. It is more about the brand message than an individual artifact. Writing differentiates Cahan & Associates from other firms. "The written word is really important," Cahan says. "Pretty work with no idea behind it just isn't enough.

In the 1961 book, *The Death and Life of Great American Cities*, urbanist Jane Jacobs examines a city's need to live and breathe and grow to be great. In her opinion, a great city needs texture, density, diversity, and dynamism. "This is an apt metaphor for branding and visual systems as well," Cahan explains. "Design ideas need to evolve and grow." This philosophy does not work with one single voice. It requires multiple talents, ideas, and techniques.

Maxygen is a leader in the optimization and modification of protein pharmaceuticals.

In 2003, world-wide annual sales of protein pharmaceuticals exceeded $32 billion.

Despite commercial success, many marketed protein pharmaceuticals have deficiencies as therapeutics.

Maxygen has four protein pharmaceuticals in development, each with blockbuster potential.

At the end of 2004, Maxygen had over $215 million in cash to advance its programs.

Maxygen has over 180 employees working to develop and commercialize improved protein pharmaceuticals.

Maxygen has over 120 U.S. and foreign patents relating to its Molecular-Breeding directed evolution platform.

Maxygen is on track to have INDs filed on two of its four product candidates in 2006.

When discussing the firm, Cahan stresses the collaborative spirit repeatedly at Cahan & Associates. Internally, they work together closely on kickoff meetings, design, and presentations. The collaborative process is driven by a combination of wanting to get to solutions quicker, and to develop better ones. Cahan finds that the staff is happier when they collaborate with each other—there is a feeling of connectedness. This healthy competition leads to more aggressive conceptual thinking. At a certain point, however, designers need to own something. They need to have control over their own project. For Cahan, collaboration is critical, and it's still an evolving work process. He says, "Sometimes, I feel like I'm building a foundation for a freeway at 60 miles (97 km) per hour, but one brick at a time."

Beyond Layout

An early lesson for a designer is that clients typically give the wrong assignment. Part of the design process is determining the correct delivery vehicle. Cahan & Associates is media agnostic. Format decisions are based on an individual basis, and they don't start a project with any preconceived notions. Cahan says, "We had a client come in requesting a leasing brochure for one of their properties. We convinced them that it would be more effective if they took key real estate 'market makers' salespeople on a Hawaiian vacation and told them about the great property for lease. That's what the client did, and it worked. Of course, we didn't make any money on that project, but later the client did come back and hire us to do additional design for them."

The debate between print and screen is a nonissue at Cahan & Associates. "There are instances where doing a print piece might be startling in a good way because it can be touched. Print feels good. It feels like home. There is a reality to it," Cahan says. "Print won't disappear. Generation Y, and beyond, may not have been brought up to revere print the way earlier generations did, but it will still exist. Technology continues to evolve, and there will always be changes in the way people seek and receive information. Rather than retreat from new technologies, Cahan addresses them directly. "Social networking is an important development in communication," he adds. "In many ways it challenges ideas about print and its appropriateness."

An improved blood-clotting factor may help patients suffering from hemophilia, trauma and shock.

An improved IFN-Gamma may provide benefits to patients with ovarian cancer, HCV and IPF.

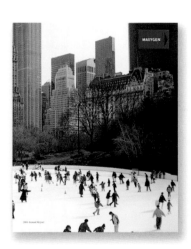

OPPOSITE AND ABOVE
As Maxygen moves closer to clinical trials, they need to communicate with broader audiences to familiarize them with the importance of Maxygen's research. Conceptually, the 2004 annual report contextualizes both the business and the human side of Maxygen's work. The effect of this elegant solution is a clear strategic positioning of Maxygen.

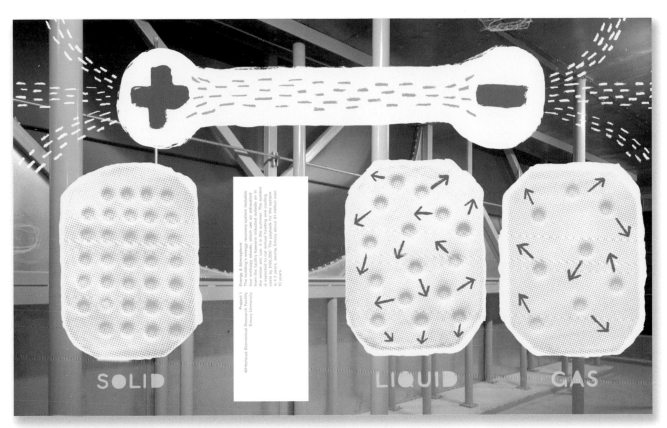

SOLID   LIQUID   GAS

Project 1
Whitehead Biomedical Research Center
Emory University

Energy & Atmosphere
The energy recovery system includes four enthalpy wheels, which use air exhausted from the facility to warm or cool incoming outside air in the winter or summer. The entire system is expected to cut annual heating and cooling costs by $105,000. The payback for the system is 4.2 years, saving Emory about $1 million over 10 years.

Researchers and designers say that biophilia is not a design fad. Groups from Harvard, Yale, and the Rocky Mountain Institute are busy attempting to quantify its effects. Simple intuition will tell you that a connection to nature is good—at work, at home, or in the wild.

CANON TODAY

Canon

Alexander Isley

Alexander Isley Inc. • Redding, Connecticut, USA ●

"I believe we are good at conveying excitement, interest, and passion," says Alexander Isley. Good design encourages a viewer to want to learn more. For this reason, Isley only works with clients who have real enthusiasm and passion for what they do. He never wants to be in a position to have to convey something that is not real. The firm works with companies and institutions to help craft their brand personalities and introduce them to the public. This happens not only by making well-crafted and powerful work, but also by using a team of designers, writers, and strategists working across multiple disciplines. This broad approach establishes a consistent voice, attitude, and point of view to position the client in the minds of the audience.

OPPOSITE
Canon Today is a series of year-in-review books providing customers, employees, and investors an overview of Canon Corporation's North American division.

Canon Today

Canon

OPPOSITE AND RIGHT
Working in association
with Canon's agency,
DCA Advertising, Isley created a series of year-end
publications. The materials
highlight Canon's products
with engaging photography
and playful typography,
rather than presenting the
products in a clinical and
information-based design.

Millions rely on Canon Quality to furnish a winning environment.

A home can be many things. A warm haven filled with the laughter of family and friends. A sanctuary from the outside world. And a highly effective working environment as well.

Canon recognizes that people work more productively in a setting where they feel more comfortable, and that great ideas aren't always governed by a time clock. By combining a full range of user needs with two more effective, compact and affordable solutions, Canon is helping people accomplish their best work at the office, even when it happens to be their home.

The Original, and Still the Best.

Remarkable Canon PC Copiers have been the leading choice of businesses and families ever since Canon originated the personal copier category. Compact enough for the desktop, they offer the perfect complement to your office. Canon's legendary...large, Neat copied every time.

A necessary companion in any home or office, today's streamlined Canon PC Copiers

The Affordable, Personal Business Link.

With its...communication function that handles incoming calls as well as transmits, Canon FAXPHONE® B160 provides a powerful communications line that doubles home office productivity. And since today's business requires performance without compromise, Canon brings the practical convenience of plain paper facsimile home with laser-quality Bubble Jet printing technology.

As advanced, hard-working examples of home-office efficiency, every Canon FAXPHONE combines the convenience

There is a FAXPHONE to answer every personal facsimile need.*

come in a wide range of user-friendly models to accommodate the particular needs of growing businesses. But by far their most important advantage is the way they deliver virtually maintenance-free performance.

For at the heart of each one is Canon's ingenious PC Cartridge, containing everything that can run out or wear out. With just a simple cartridge replacement, it's almost like getting a new copier in return.

of telephone and facsimile into a single personal-sized unit that takes up a minimum of operating space. The fact is, the innovative Canon FAXPHONE line is designed to handle every facsimile job effortlessly and economically. Compact and portable, they're the last word in personal business communication.

With an outstanding line that also extends to personal typewriters, personal word processors, and desktop calculators, Canon's Home Office Products provide a glimpse into the unlimited potential of today's changing workstyle. Because from any office, from any setting, the performance tools of Canon give more people the ability to accomplish their best.

Sleek new PC-300 Series Copiers provide the utmost in reliability.

Experience the quality of a constantly refined image.

It is there only for an instant. A moment when lighting and mood combine to create an image that is truly priceless. At Canon, being able to secure that fleeting image is the essence of great photography, and is the focus of all our efforts.

By constantly finding ways to make professional quality images more accessible to everyone, Canon envisions a world of photography and video making that captures the real world just as it is, or however one chooses to reveal it.

Capturing Every Moment's Meaning.

When it comes to expressing the full impact of an image and its meaning, **Canon Cameras** secure it with exceptional subtlety and sharpness. For whatever the photographer's eye witnesses, Canon can capture.

Whether the person behind the camera is an accomplished professional or a beginner makes little difference to Canon. Each is trying to preserve the subject or occasion exactly as it appears, and with every snap of the shutter, that's what Canon delivers. Knowing that Canon can faithfully reproduce the images of the mind's eye gives professionals the confidence to pursue their unique vision. And for amateurs of all

Canon 8mm camcorders offer the perfect blend of automated ease and advanced features.

levels of ability, Canon's innovative technology provides an effortless way to achieve outstanding results.

Putting affordable, high-quality picture taking within everyone's reach is a Canon legacy that continues to this day. Sturdy, lightweight cameras like the Canon Snappy and Sure Shot provide an affordable entry

able to envision

into the world of 35mm photography, while the best-selling EOS Rebel series brings the benefits of advanced autofocus SLR operation to an even greater number of new users. And in the latest example of camera evolution, Canon's exclusive Eye Controlled Focus technology enables the EOS A2E to instantly focus on the photographer's line of sight.

Steady Performers.

In the quest for continuous product improvement, Canon has always provided a steady source of innovation, and **Canon 8mm Video Camcorders** are no exception. For years, people have grown to rely on their automatic

operation and superior image quality. For Canon's latest models even correct such difficulties as camcorder shake. Because an Optical Image Stabilizer that omits the slightest unwanted movement and counteracts it instantly, using unique Canon technology to produce clear, stable recordings.

Ultra compact, and capable of intense resolution, Canon camcorders now offer ergonomically shaped bodies for hours of

fatigue-free shooting. But it is their unquestioned ability to capture life's simple moments that makes them the choice of a growing number of video enthusiasts.

In the uncompromising art of image making where others merely focus on the world, Canon is able to envision their vision.

EOS A2E, the world's first camera with Eye Controlled Focus.

Canon Index, 1994.

WIIO ARE
YOU?

...the past couple of years, there's been a lot ...timistic talk about Interactive media. ...'s seems to us as foolish as the overblown ...sm that gripped the industry before that. ... take a much more settled view. A ...ic view. A *business* view.

...t's how we helped a well-known airline ... the online leader in sales and service. ...laced their online messaging efforts with ...ation and utilities customers wanted. ...en we developed a plan to migrate

customers from expensive live interactions to digital sales and support. Today they're selling a ticket every 10 seconds on their Web site—while reducing service costs by as much as 85 percent.

What did it take for them to achieve such spectacular results? They were willing to make a long-term commitment, putting their whole company behind the effort.

And, if we may say so, they chose the right Interactive Marketing partner.

OPPOSITE AND ABOVE
Communications materials for Modem Media are aimed at C-level potential clients, providing an overview of Modem Media, a pioneer in digital marketing and communication. Modem Media's strengths include the development of sophisticated websites for Fortune 500 companies.

The *Move Me* publication is approached with a skeptical consumer's point of view. The message is told in the first person across a series of provocative spreads. Isley believes that clients who are experts in communication often need to go to outside to tell their own stories.

Chevron Texaco needed a commemorative publication celebrating the 100th Anniversary of Texaco. The company has extensive archives relating to their history of exploration, marketing, and philanthropy, and they wanted a keepsake book for all employees, investors, and friends of the company. Isley met with the company's archivists and explored the thousands of items in their collection. The book is oversized, lavishly illustrated, and includes a poster showcasing the evolution of the iconic Texaco "star" logo. A special, limited-edition, leather-bound version of the book exists. Although Texaco merged with the Chevron Corporation during production, the book is a definitive history of Texaco.

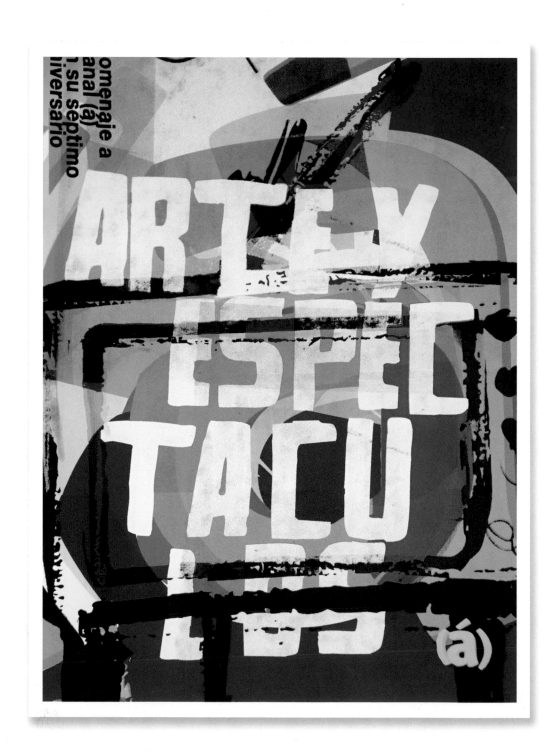

Guillermo Stein

Steinbranding • Buenos Aires, Argentina

Listening to the client is the core philosophy at Steinbranding. Principal Guillermo Stein adheres to the mandate of switching off the inner dialogue we have as designers. "If I listen to him, I understand him. If I understand, I am able to do my work better," Stein says of his client relationships. Communicating a message is a very difficult task and it demands responsibility. Stein's approach of listening and connecting is the first step.

OPPOSITE
These posters for Elgourmet.com are designed as a piece of art as a premium for each of the main channels distributed by Pramer. After a period of research, Steinbranding designed the art for six serigraphies to be produced by a special artist.

> "Only when designers free themselves from the need of applause will they be able to produce successful pieces."
>
> —Guillermo Stein

Contradictory Messages

The work produced at Steinbranding is kinetic, vibrant, and aggressive. The visual energy is at odds with Stein's clear and well-mannered personal interaction. His calm demeanor—combined with his ability to listen and synthesize what is actually being said—creates work that stands apart from the norm.

Many of Steinbranding's projects begin as broadcast or motion design. The challenge is to take the criteria developed and create a communication that relies on movement and sound, then apply it to a static, printed form. Having a clear vision and direction maintains a cohesive message in both media. "Each format and medium has its own energy and produces different effects on people," says Stein. "To define that effect, I put myself in the shoes of the people who'll get the piece and try to feel what emotions the product triggers in me."

Losing the aspect of sound and time could lead to certain failure. Stein overcomes this challenge and makes it an advantage. The printed matter is not just a still image from the motion piece. It is typically an evolution of the idea. The message is deliberately maintained, and the kinetic nature of motion translates to work that is dimensional and allows the viewer to create the movement and sound in his own head. Stein does not think of printed matter as a 2-D form, but as a 3-D window with elements in a spatial field. This is literally apparent in a project such as the Discovery Kids Zootrope, a toy with a series of images on the inner surface of a cylinder. As the cylinder is rotated and viewed through a series of slits, it gives the impression of continuous motion.

Pollution

For Stein, print media is still perceived as more reliable. Unfortunately, the web and interactive world is so "polluted" that it's necessary to work harder to filter the useful information for a client. "The distribution of print materials cannot be compared to that of electronic media. Electronic media offers an infinite possibility of flooding the globe with its communication, while print media is distributed by hand," Stein says. A positive aspect of print communication is that the viewer must take time and hold the piece. Print materials can also be borrowed and lent. It is possible to share a website address with a friend, but more meaningful to hand him a booklet. Stein says, "This makes print materials unique."

OPPOSITE
The serigraphy reflects the spirit of Elgourmet.com, the most popular lifestyle Latin American channel throughout the continent, in a highly artistic way. Everything from the paper to the number of each to be produced is taken into account. The posters are not produced in large quantities and have become coveted objects.

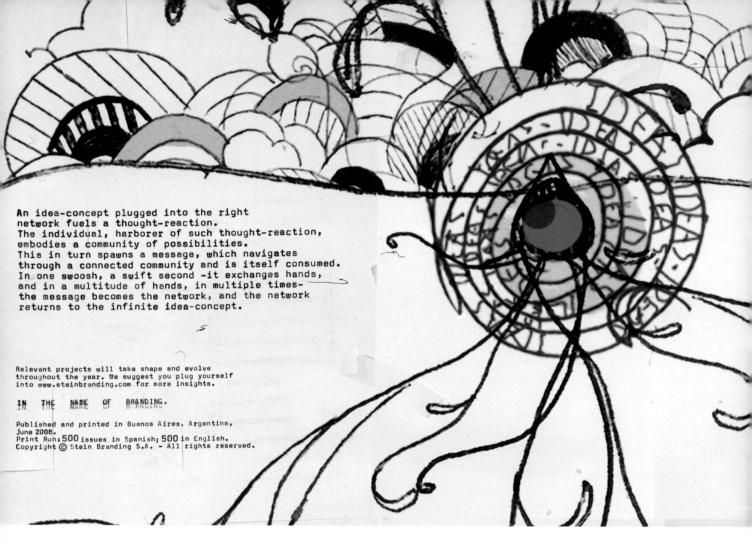

An idea-concept plugged into the right
network fuels a thought-reaction.
The individual, harborer of such thought-reaction,
embodies a community of possibilities.
This in turn spawns a message, which navigates
through a connected community and is itself consumed.
In one swoosh, a swift second -it exchanges hands,
and in a multitude of hands, in multiple times-
the message becomes the network, and the network
returns to the infinite idea-concept.

Relevant projects will take shape and evolve
throughout the year. We suggest you plug yourself
into www.steinbranding.com for more insights.

IN THE NAME OF BRANDING.

Published and printed in Buenos Aires, Argentina,
June 2008.
Print Run: 500 issues in Spanish; 500 in English.

"The main characteristic of print communications that fail is when they are not properly adapted to the format," explains Stein. Templates are useful and provide consistency but fail when they are used with no regard for the individual message. A newspaper or magazine ad that is adapted to a billboard is a good example. "To maintain consistency throughout several pieces, I avoid systematic adaptations. Each piece has a particular use," he says. Stein also addresses ego as an ingredient for failure. "Another reason for failure is when being creative takes priority over the communication. Only when designers free themselves from the need of applause will they be able to produce successful pieces."

Simple Advice

Stein's approach is direct and logical. "First, write down the goals that are being sought by the project. Then build a model or mock-up as close as possible to the finished product. Test the solution among colleagues, friends, and relatives. And really listen to their criticism. Finally, reread what you've written and ask yourself if there is a better way to solve it."

Sustainable practices have proven challenging for Stein in Argentina. "Unfortunately, there's not a complete awareness on these subjects. Many of the clients still don't focus on these matters, " he says. For the time being, Steinbranding has addressed this need by replacing some of the print communication like style guides with electronic communication.

"The most challenging aspect of corporate communication is seeing everything printed and delivered, and to maintain the same vision as when the project started," says Stein. Steinbranding maintains communication with the client throughout the process and is direct about results once the project concludes. They look at sales revenue increases, ratings, and other business aspects that affect a client's success.

qqmqQuick look at situations
that come up as we survey the MARKET:

****

EXT. - NIGHT

Interviewer: "Mr. Smith, what do you think
                                about this logo?"
Consumer: "Mmmh... can't read the small print"

**

Interviewer: "Do you like the ergonomic pack?"
Consumer: "Are these giveaways?"

*
*

Interviewer: "And what do you think of the logo now?"
Consumer: "Now it looks upside-down!"
                                        pommu

*
*

Interviewer: "Without any effort, what brand
                                first comes to your mind?"
Consumer: "I don't know, something fancy..."

**OPPOSITE, ABOVE,
AND RIGHT**
In the Name of Branding,
is a publication that is
not aimed at any specific
client. The goal is to
generate controversy
around the designer's
everyday work. It is to
question what branding

in communications is.
The publication posits the
idea that everybody talks
about branding, but do we
really know precisely what
it is and what it means?

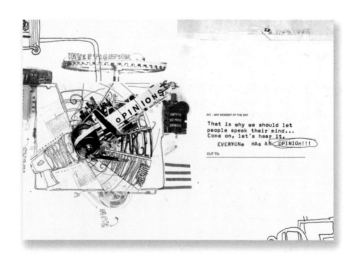

ABOVE AND OPPOSITE
The Ministry of Education
of Argentina commissioned
Steinbranding to create
the brand for a new
educational television
channel. Encuentro's logo
incorporates an equal sign
as its most outstanding

feature. This is a synthesis
of the idea of education
and equality. Encuentro
is now regarded as the
new educational examplar.

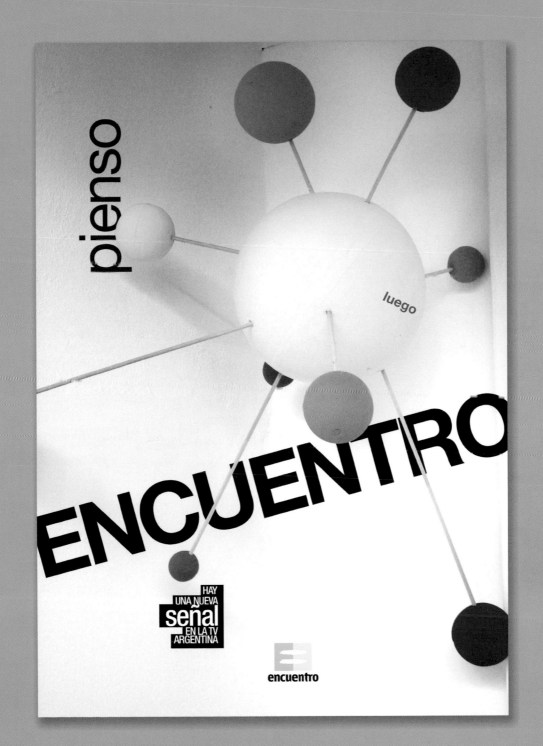

KUHLMANN LEAVITT, INC.
ST. LOUIS, MISSOURI, USA

LEFT
Deanna Kuhlmann-Leavitt

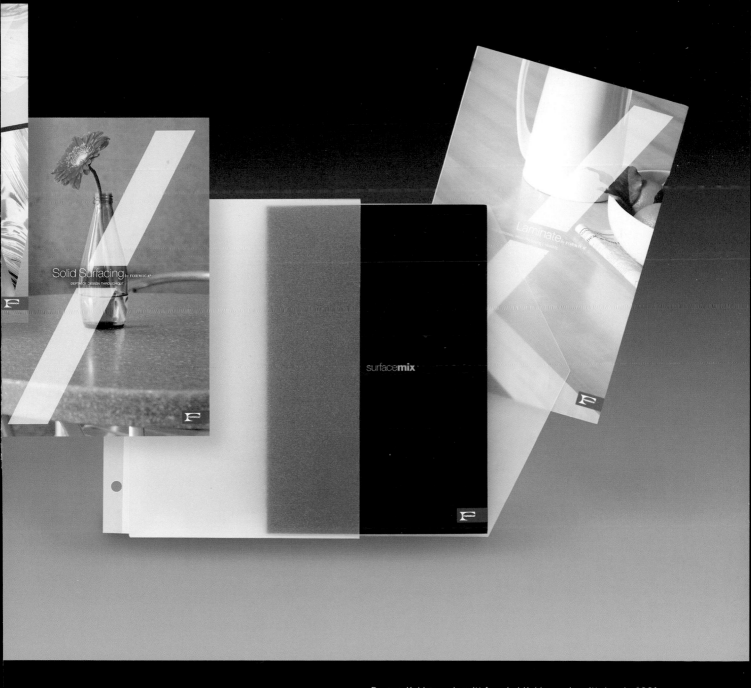

Deanna Kuhlmann-Leavitt founded Kuhlmann Leavitt, Inc. in 2001.
Kuhlmann-Leavitt and her staff educate themselves about the
client's business, and work to further the client's business objectives.
At the same time, they create work that is fresh, intelligent, and clear.
Kuhlmann Leavitt is one of the highest regarded firms in the United
States, but they humbly state, "We do good work."

ABOVE AND
PAGES 142–143
In celebration of the combinations and juxtapositions that can be created with Formica products, Deanna Kuhlmann-Leavitt conceived a book that's designed to inspire architects and designers. The book itself is a rich exploration of texture and color, utilizing various glossy and uncoated papers and describes all the environments and ways in which Formica products are used: Live/Work, Care/Host, Play/Learn, Shop/Dine, Green/Good. In each section, the photography serves to spark ideas for innovative ways to design surfaces in all sorts of interiors. Scattered throughout are whimsical, intricate typographic illustrations that support and enhance the content.

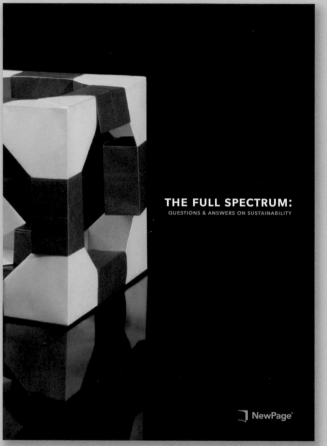

THE FULL SPECTRUM:
QUESTIONS & ANSWERS ON SUSTAINABILITY

NewPage®

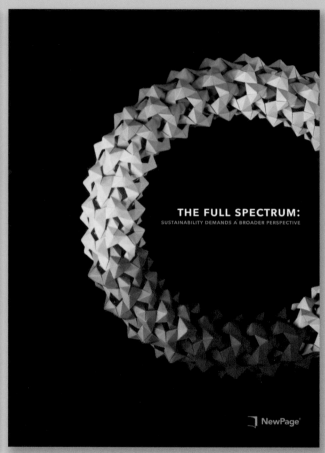

THE FULL SPECTRUM:
SUSTAINABILITY DEMANDS A BROADER PERSPECTIVE

NewPage®

SPEAK UP. SAVE LIVES

anonymously report weapon threats

1-866-SPEAK-UP

speak up!

pax
Real Solutions to Gun
www.paxusa

Stephen Doyle

A project created by Doyle Partners is typically fresh, direct, harmonious, and has a layer of intelligence and wit. Partner Stephen Doyle has maintained the same vision for twenty years. As he says, "The most important thing about communicating a client's message is to help them figure out what the hell it is." For Doyle, client's minds are like coral reefs, and they build up a little calcium day after day, and after a few years, they become a great hiding ground for very colorful fish with imaginative shapes. He uses this analogy to describe one of his goals: "The fish need to be coaxed out of hiding, and they are very slippery."

OPPOSITE
Pax is an organization devoted to stopping gun violence, without getting entangled in the constitutional arguments of rights and wrongs. Two platforms comprise the organization: "Ask" is an initiative to prompt parents to ask if there is a gun where their children are playing (at the homes of neighbors or friends). The second leg is "Speak Up," an anonymous phone number for school kids to call in case they hear about a weapon threat.

CHJ Northside High School

Welcome Students

SCHOOL SHOOTING
IN THE LIBRARY
10:00 AM TOMORROW

In 4 out of 5 school shootings
the attackers tell other students first.
The signs are usually there.
Now there's something you can do.
Call 1-866-SPEAK-UP
to anonymously report a weapon threat.

speak up!

pax
Real Solutions to Gun Violence
www.paxusa.org

SPEAK UP. SAVE LIVES.
1-866-SPEAK-UP

Real Story

Celia, Idaho

In September, a student told Celia he was planning a massacre at school. Celia spoke up. It turned out he had an AK-47 assault rifle, hundreds of rounds of ammunition, hunting knives, and even bombs. Celia's courageous call prevented a senseless tragedy and probably saved many innocent lives.

Want to get more involved?

• keep this in your wallet
• share it with your friends
• bring SPEAK UP to your school
• write a letter to your local newspaper
• design a SPEAK UP poster or t-shirt

For more ideas, visit:
www.speakup.com
or email speakup@paxusa.org

speak up!

SPEAK UP. Save lives.
Call 1-866-SPEAK-UP.
It's anonymous and free.

Did you know?

In 4 out of 5 school shootings, the attackers tell other students about their plans.

Now there's something you can do...

If you know about a student carrying a weapon at school, or threatening violence with a weapon,...

• Don't assume it's a joke!

• Don't try to handle it yourself!

• Tell a teacher or trusted adult, or...

...CALL
1-866-SPEAK-UP
It's anonymous and free.

OVER 10,000 CALLS LAST YEAR

Sometimes, it is the assumptions of the industry, the talk of the trade, or the old habits that obscure the real message from your client. The client is a designer's partner in a project. It is important for the designer to communicate the way that outsiders view—and experience—the client's brand, products, or services. "Being naive about the projects that I embark on is one of the best assets I bring to a project," says Doyle. "After I hear someone's spiel, I inevitably start with this line: 'Can I ask a really stupid question?'" After hammering away at the client's assumptions and predispositions, Doyle then is ready to actually uncover what the message should be. He then determines a thorough understanding of the context where the message will be seen. It is only after these issues have been explored that he will start thinking about design. And he maintains this philosophy: "When designing, it's not about *you*, it's about *them*."

There is no single format used repeatedly at Doyle Partners. Doyle believes the format should be just as small as it can be, no

smaller, or just as big as it can be, no bigger. Everything in between is a waste. He incorporates an online presence as an invaluable tool, but finds that printing can be a better way to attract attention. "Beware the difference between print-outs and print," and he adds, "Print is a nice way to actually emphasize the beauty of a printed object as a object." For instance, a letterpressed business card actually talks to a viewer's fingertips. This is a connective and tactile experience that is useful when most of your communication is digital. Excellent printing can bring a higher level of professionalism, especially if a client is working out of the garage.

Authority

Print confers authority. Doyle landed his first job at *Esquire* magazine after graduating from Cooper Union. He recalls, "When I returned home to Lutherville, Maryland, the neighbors advanced on me, excitement on their faces, their arms outstretched. They said, 'I saw your name in the magazine!' It was remarkable that the printing of my name, in 8-point type on

ABOVE AND OPPOSITE
This identity uses the metaphor of transparency and overlap to indicate the structure of Pax. Each program has an identity appropriate to its audience. It is a priority at Doyle Partners to create pro bono work for these types of imaginative programs with critical impact.

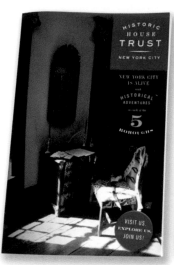

1. Use correct grammar. An email or a text is not a printed communication. "Gr8 2 C U!" is fine for that, but printing is language incarnate. Use it correctly.

2. When in doubt, leave it out. If something doesn't need to be said, don't say it. If an image does not enhance your understanding or delight, get rid of it. If something does not need to be printed, don't print it.

3. Get the printer to take the magenta down a little bit—especially in those faces over there on the right. And color correct in daylight. Forget those stupid boxes with the weird lights. (And make sure you do color correct.)

4. Don't design square mailers for nonprofit clients, especially if they are soliciting money via some event or dinner for which I have to pay to go and eat chicken, because the postage is more for both the mailer and the reply, and who in their right mind would want to give extra money to the U.S. Postal Service? Square invitations make designers look stupid. Oh, that and "Please RSVP." If anyone needs this explained, call Sean Adams at home anytime of day or night.

5. Gee, I always forget the fifth rule.

60-lb. stock, and distributed in the mail could somehow, in their eyes, validate me, the same kid who grew up down the block. That is the power of print."

Doyle equates problematic functionality with communications that fail. "I think 'Free Kittens' flyers with a tear-off phone number tab at the bottom are failures. Usually all the tabs are still there on the bottom, and the thing has been on the telephone pole so long those cute little meowing kittens have all probably turned into horrible overweight cats with bad habits."

Doyle also finds consistency to be overrated. He believes consistency and logic are made out to seem more than they are worth. The omnipotence of a huge global brand is in many cases the antithesis of what people are looking for today, when microbrews and local products are raising awareness and pride and all kinds of issues about the wonderful differences that keep us interesting (and interested). Doyle says, "There is a Chinese tailor near my home in the Village, and he has a sign in his window that says, 'If we all looked alike, how could we fall in love?'" His time at Tibor Kalman's noted design firm, M & Co., taught him an important lesson: "Why have a personality if you're not going to use it? Brands need to learn how

to have personalities, not guidelines. They need to learn how to modulate their voices. In the same way that people dress, they express their personalities through clothing, and they wear vastly different clothing for different occasions," he explains. But it is usually faithful to the core personality, even though beachwear is vastly different from work, weddings, or car washing. Although Doyle admits, he has some clients for whom "work" and "car washing" are a pretty tough call. Doyle Partners' work demonstrates it is the feeling of a voice or a personality that makes a brand hold together visually—it is a consistency of approach, not solution, that allows a brand to breathe.

"Right now, I'm working on a design for the Band-Aid box at the same time I am designing a fritting pattern for a skyscraper in Toronto that is a quarter of a mile high," Doyle says. His enthusiasm for design is apparent in the variety of work the firm creates. "The great thing about design is that there are tons of different formats, and each can be used to tell a different story to a different audience. And that is my favorite thing, to romp between scales, materials, locations, and audiences, using design to spread information, exercise ideas, and enchant."

ABOVE AND OPPOSITE
Historic House Trust is a
consortium of twenty-two
houses and buildings in
New York City that are
owned and run by the
Department of Parks.
From different ages, with
different architecture and
diverse geography, they
tell part of the history
of New York City. Doyle
Partners' contribution to
their image was to visit
all the sites with a good

camera and a curious
eye, shooting at will with
natural light and a tourist's
enthusiasm. The logo
recalls trade type from the
nineteenth century, the
different fonts alluding to
the diverse collection of
structures and the stories
they each tell. The bright
color of the logo was
actually derived from the
interior of a cabinet in
the Van Cortland House,
built in 1748.

My Building
Saves Energy,
Water...
and Money.
That's Green.
7 World Trade Center earned a Gold LEED rating from the U.S. Green Building Council. Using rainwater for secondary plumbing functions is just one of many things Silverstein Properties did to make 7WTC green. I know, because I'm the engineer. You know because USGBC's LEED certification confirms it.
Immediate savings.
Measurable results.
LEED delivers green.
Learn how: USGBC.org
U.S. GREEN BUILDING COUNCIL
USGBC
Steve Nathan, Chief Engineer, 7WTC
7WTC was developed by Silverstein Properties

"When you *do* see your clients face to face,
it's a good thing to have your shoes polished.
And get some hard leather shoes, and shine them."

—**Stephen Doyle**

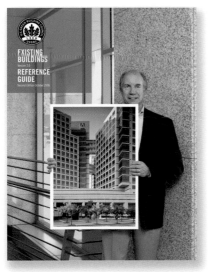

ABOVE AND OPPOSITE
When USGBC (United States Green Building Council) asked Doyle Partners to help them reposition their marketing materials, the job came with one warning: "Don't touch the logo!" Naturally, Doyle ignored them. They reconfigured the logo to serve as a translation of their anagram, spelling out U.S. Green Building Council on the top, and summarizing USGBC on the bottom. They had some vague leaves in a circle before, but these were altered to oak leaves, representing a strong building material as well as a typically American tree.

Doyle Partners ✳ 157

opendialogue
FONTS & FUNCTIONALITY

OPEN DiALOgUE

Adobe

GET OPEN

Bill Grant

Grant Design Collaborative • Canton, Georgia, USA

There are some designers who believe that work must be hard to be good. Any result that is not the product of hair pulling and all-night work sessions must be bad. The solutions tend to reflect this attitude and are often overwrought and desperate. Grant Design Collaborative founder, Bill Grant, may spend arduous hours with his team on a project, but the final result always has an air of inevitability. The message and form seem to have landed in exactly the right spot, and there is no other solution. Grant explains, "In order to figure out what role print pieces will play in the brand strategy, we ask: 'What are we trying to communicate? What is it about the brand we are trying to say? And, what is best way to do this with the least amount of effort?' The path of least resistance is usually the most effective."

OPPOSITE
The Adobe Font Magalog is a cross between a magazine and a catalog. Grant created this publication to showcase Adobe's Fonts. By exploring a playful dynamic made only Adobe typefaces, he proves the flexibility and variety of the product.

Grant Design Collaborative's materials for Herman Miller support the objectives to be human, spirited, and purposeful. The holiday greeting extends the company's giving program by allowing designers and architects to select one of four charities to have a contribution made in their name. Organizations range from the Design Industries Foundation Fighting AIDS to Habitat for Humanity. The large poster perforates into sheets of gift wrap to further increase awareness of the charitable organizations.

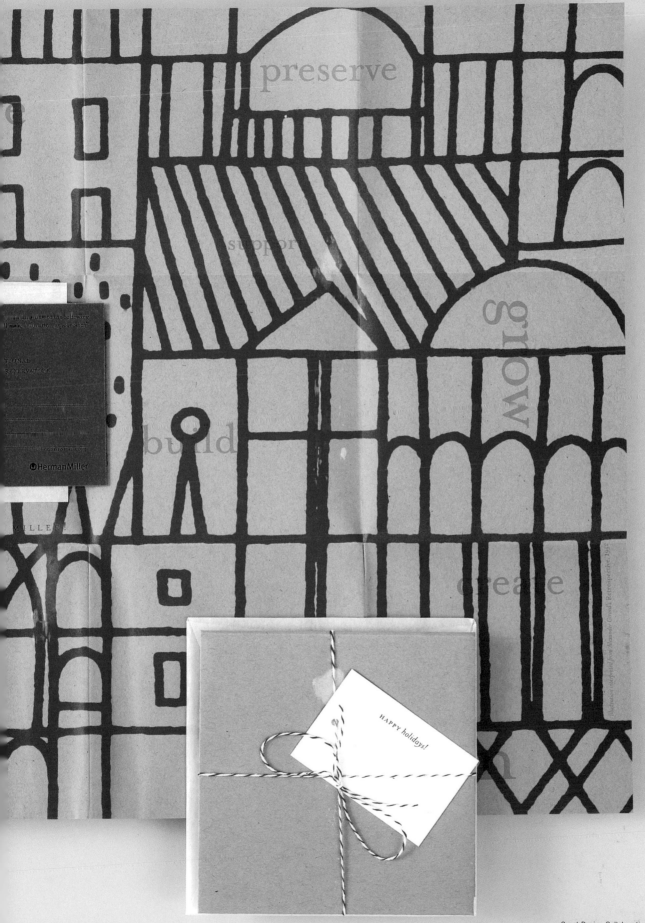

preserve

support

grow

build

create

HAPPY holidays!

HermanMiller

insight

IN

Blueridge

Blue Ridge Commercial Carpet
Ellijay, Georgia 800.241.5945   04042

Blue Ridge Commercial
Carpet is a specialty
manufacturer of uniquely
designed and engineered
commercial carpet. For
over thirty years, Blue
Ridge has produced
durable and stylish carpet
for a wide variety of
commercial installations.

The products are created
by a highly-motivated team
of artists and craftsmen
who live and work in the
Blue Ridge Mountains.
Grant followed the com-
pany's values, that design
is everything, everything is
design, and a commitment
to their our own community
as the driving concepts to
create engaging materials.

"Designers need to look beyond the question 'what's in it for me?'"

—Bill Grant

that piece." He says, "It always shocks me that they've kept it. Some things are just covetable. If you do a good job, people sense the value. If it has value, it's not disposable."

Green-wash

Making artifacts that will not be disposable is at the core of Grant's sustainable practices. The green issue is relatively important to his clients, and recently their interest has increased. For each project, using FSC-certified papers, inks, and printers is explored. For Grant Design Collaborative, the cost is worth the result. Modern consumers value sustainability. "There is a lot of 'green washing' going on out there—people doing things for the wrong reasons," explains Grant, "This aspect is evolving rapidly. We are diligent about educating the team at Grant Design Collaborative and our clients about sustainability. We're looking at innovations that can help us make more with less."

If making more with less is a factor in successful projects, indulgence by the designer is one of the most commonalities with failed projects. A piece fails for Grant when it becomes more about the design than the message. "We write 95 percent of our work," Grant says. "It starts with the written word. No piece will be effective if it's beautiful to look at, but the copy isn't cohesive." Grant will not allow budget to be the excuse. He has made a

priority to understand budget restrictions, then design the best piece possible within those parameters. It's rare to hear a client say, "I have too much money and too much time." But Grant maintains you can have the biggest budget in the world and still not be effective. Regardless of budget, he always asks these questions: "How do you communicate in an overbranded world? How do you maintain quality and continue to innovate? How do you do great design consistently?"

Process

Each design firm has its own way of working. There are a multitude of styles and processes to get the job done. At Grant Design Collaborative, they handle everything. Grant rarely uses freelance people and has built a consistent team that has been together for years. He works to keep turnover at a minimum. One key component of the successful process is the creation of a Brand Resource Team for each client. He explains, "We don't just assign one person to work with a client. The entire team spends time developing a Brand Roadmap or strategy that results in a Vision Book for each client. We create war rooms and all post ideas, thoughts, and strategies. We present them to each other and together put everything through a filter based on the needs of a client. Then we assign a team leader, a brand resource manager, who could be a designer or a strategist—we don't have account executives."

The designers talk directly to clients. Grant removes as many layers as possible. The brand resource manager makes sure that everything stays on message and on brand, and the firm is small enough so Grant can review everything. He has put a system in place to maintain the basic structure and ensure consistency. This leads to long-term contracts with clients. Building a strong team demands a clear vision and philosophy. Mentoring and educating the team is as important as maintaining the computer system. For Grant, the advice comes easily. "If a designer wants to do successful work, listen to the client. One thing that drives me crazy with young designers is how much it is all about them and not their clients. They need to listen and think about what needs to be designed," he says. "Before jumping into design, start by sketching concepts before going to the computer. Also, check your ego at the door. Do great work, push your clients where and when appropriate." Grant explains that the time to push the client is when it is critical to communicate a message or brand, and not just visually. The ongoing success and world-class work created by his team is the result of truly listening, not just jumping to a new visual effect. In the end, Grant sums up his philosophy succinctly, "Being creative means considering form and function."

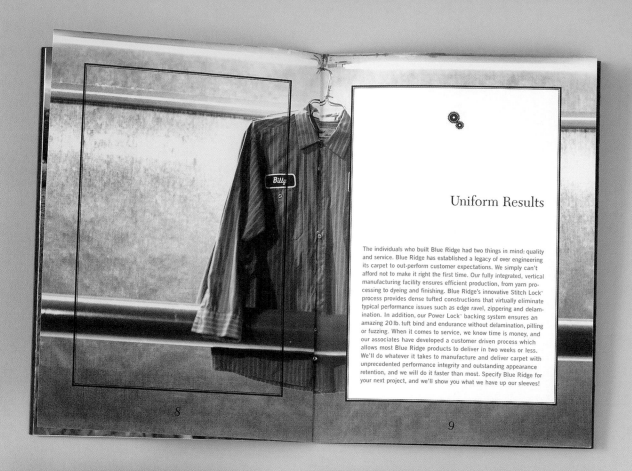

Uniform Results

The individuals who built Blue Ridge had two things in mind: quality and service. Blue Ridge has established a legacy of over engineering its carpet to out-perform customer expectations. We simply can't afford not to make it right the first time. Our fully integrated, vertical manufacturing facility ensures efficient production, from yarn processing to dyeing and finishing. Blue Ridge's innovative Stitch Lock™ process provides dense tufted constructions that virtually eliminate typical performance issues such as edge ravel, zippering and delamination. In addition, our Power Lock™ backing system ensures an amazing 20 lb. tuft bind and endurance without delamination, pilling or fuzzing. When it comes to service, we know time is money, and our associates have developed a customer driven process which allows most Blue Ridge products to deliver in two weeks or less. We'll do whatever it takes to manufacture and deliver carpet with unprecedented performance integrity and outstanding appearance retention, and we will do it faster than most. Specify Blue Ridge for your next project, and we'll show you what we have up our sleeves!

8

9

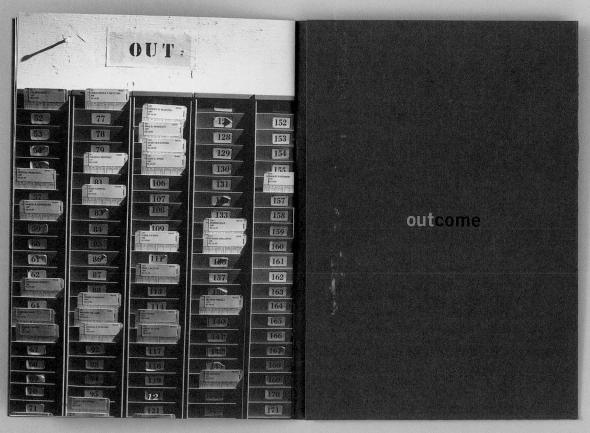

Time and Place

In the rolling foothills of the Appalachian Mountains, the Ellijay River merges with the Cartecay to form the Coosawattee in the small town of Ellijay, Georgia - a place the Cherokee tribe labeled "land of many waters." In some respects, the area has escaped many of the trappings of modern life. The town square contains antique merchants, a barber shop, a gallery of local art, a pool room, a coffee house and a few surprises. Ellijay is known as the "Apple Capital of the South," and family orchards produce over a dozen varieties each year. The growing season culminates in an apple harvest festival each fall. We are a proud community of honest, hard-working men and women who still know the basic difference between right and wrong. Most days in Ellijay seem a little Norman Rockwell. Throw in some Twin Peaks eccentricity for good measure, and there you have it. It is in this context that we live and work. This is the place where we make Blue Ridge Commercial Carpet.

3

A Product of Our Environment

Blue Ridge appreciates the power of design. Our inspiration comes in a variety of forms, from our beautiful location in the foothills of the Blue Ridge mountains to the arts and crafts heritage of our community. In fact, Blue Ridge is becoming a virtual gallery of design talent. We utilize an eclectic mixture of award-winning independent product designers to create original combinations of color, texture and pattern in a variety of forms. Just take a look at some of our latest product collections, and you'll discover a classic, hand-crafted style that distinguishes Blue Ridge carpet from the "me-too" design mentality. When it comes to custom products, we must admit that our manufacturing agility comes in handy. For instance, many of our products can be custom colored for a low minimum of 45 feet. Blue Ridge also produces custom patterns, textures and weights on a routine basis. While some may consider Blue Ridge to be a boutique mill, we prefer to think of ourselves in more modest terms. Our products are designed to perform beautifully in a wide variety of commercial environments. We have no interest in being pigeon-holed. If you need it, we'll make it, and we prefer to keep it that simple.

7

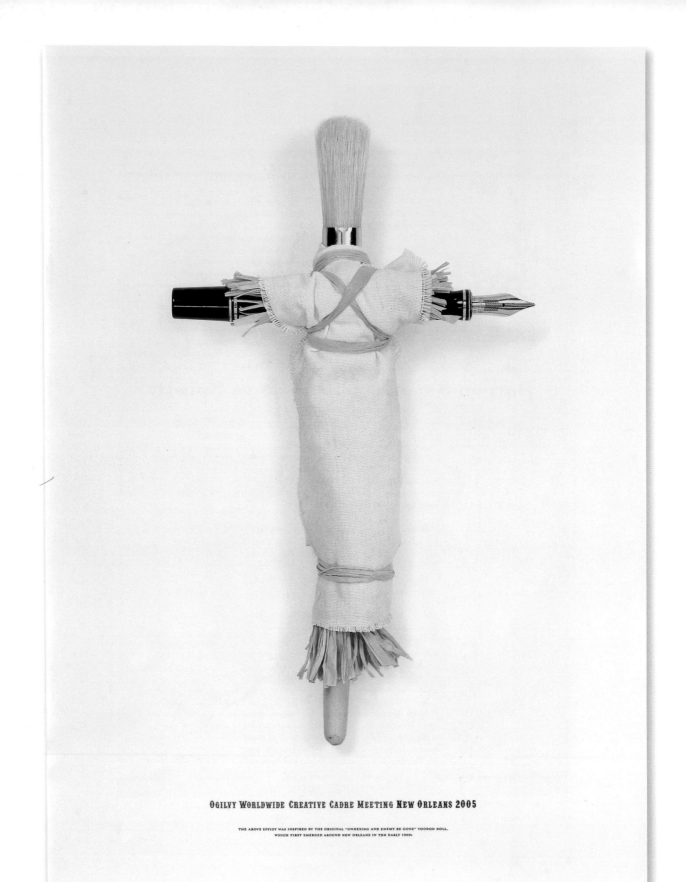

OGILVY WORLDWIDE CREATIVE CADRE MEETING NEW ORLEANS 2005

THE ABOVE EFFIGY WAS INSPIRED BY THE ORIGINAL "UNHEXING AND ENEMY BE GONE" VOODOO DOLL,
WHICH FIRST EMERGED AROUND NEW ORLEANS IN THE EARLY 1900s

Garth Walker

● **Mister Walker** • Durban, South Africa

Mister Walker founder, Garth Walker, says, "We're just
ordinary people who truly love design and want to share
the magic." He prides himself on not being slick or trendy.
He is not interested in making complex bars and charts,
heavy-handed creative rationales, or using oblique "design
speak." Walker is interested in "what it looks like," he
says. He follows this by forming genuine partnerships with
his clients, working for the long term, and staying lean.
But in the end, he succeeds at helping a client move to
a better place. The message is a vital part of the client's
success. "Generally, the message is determined by both
studio and client. We offer insights here, as some clients
aren't sure of the 'what and the how,'" says Walker.

PAGE 170 AND ABOVE
The newsletter/congress momento was produced for Ogilvy Worldwide Creative Cadre Meeting held in New Orleans. The newsletter reflects the event, people, images, and an overview of discussions.

In addition, some spreads are devoted to senior Ogilvy Worldwide creatives who were free to express "whatever." The cover depicts an art spoof on a traditional New Orleans voodoo doll.

He factors in the audience and the medium, and asks three questions suggested to him by Milton Glaser: "Who are we talking to? What do we want to tell them? How do we want to say it?" Walker says, "These always work for me."

Touching

Walker is not, in his words, "a web guy." Consequently, print will always be his first choice. For Walker, print is tactile. The reader can feel it, smell it, and read it anywhere; he can keep it, throw it away, and carry it. "You can use it for other stuff, like starting a barbecue. And one day it may end up in a design book and is remembered as a great piece," he says. "Interactive is only for teenagers (and they eventually grow out of it)."

Walker's favorite projects are defined not by a specific form or design, but if the whole project was a pleasure. In his experience, it is easy to lose enthusiasm for a project when the client or printer becomes problematic. "All great work needs be fun at every step. I like the projects that enable me to push my boundaries or find a new way of saying what I want to say," Walker notes. Alternatively, the common experience of projects that fail is when the viewer says, "Huh? Errr what's this?"—when it's impossible to understand. "And there's quite a lot of it out there— the designer's ego got in the way," he says. It's rarely a result of bad printing or the wrong paper.

Politics and Design

For Walker, African clients are behind the global issues such as sustainable practices. He finds that most African designers' response is to simply print on recycled paper. At Mister Walker, he tries to keep the green process realistic in this environment. Currently, this requires more green education than actually producing sustainable printed matter. This is one example of the most challenging component of a project. "For us, it's keeping the people factor under control. Most corporations have political dynamics that have nothing to do with design dynamics," says Walker. Some designers are better suited for this than others. "Personally, I prefer to work with individuals than groups," he says.

Like Glaser, Walker has a set of directives to guide himself and others: do personal work at all costs, find something you like doing and do well, and never ever give up, and the work we do to pay the bills is not what we will be remembered for. And most importantly, "go with your heart, park the ego, and always remember, this is never easy."

BELOW
Until his death in 2006,
Kunene was South Africa's
only poet laureate and
a widely acclaimed writer.
The Mazisi Kunene Foun-
dation was established
as a foundation to promote
and encourage African
literature and writing
in indigenous languages.
This project was used
to launch the foundation
and is a facsimile of
Mazisi's unpublished
poetry in a limited-
ediiton booklet. Number
one in the edition was
auctioned internationally
and succeeded in raising
significant funds for
the foundation.

SAINTE-ETIENNE

L'ENFANT JESUS

ABOVE
The series of posters looks at an African perspective on the city of Saint-Etienne in the year 2036. The issues are HIV/AIDS as a global pandemic, the continued dependency on foreign aid, the futility of the arms race, the history of Saint-Etienne as an armaments manufacturer, an African view on the G8 group and their continued exploitation of Africa, and the escalating War on Terror.

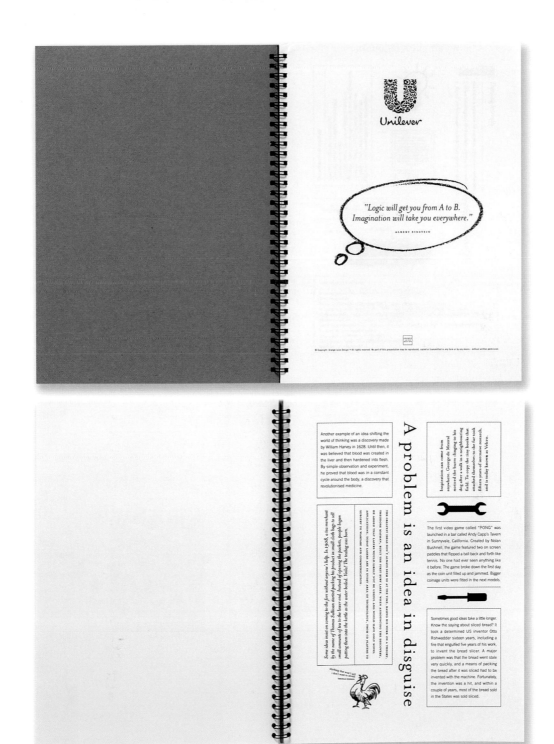

ABOVE

This booklet aimed at Unilever's marketing personnel is designed to encourage creative thinking. The content is a selection of interesting facts, mind puzzles, and visual tricks.

Following South Africa's
democratic elections in
1994, the new government
elected to commission the
building of the Constitu-
tional Court of South Africa
as a monument to the new
constitution. The court
judges commissioned a
typeface to be designed
for exclusive use within
the interior and exterior
of the building. The
content of the book
describes the creation
of the Constitutional
Court's typeface.

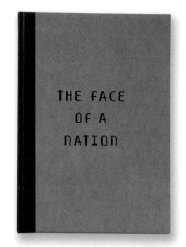

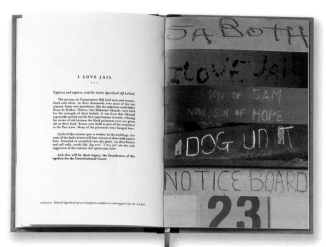

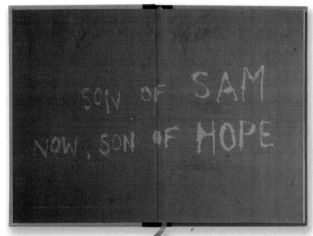

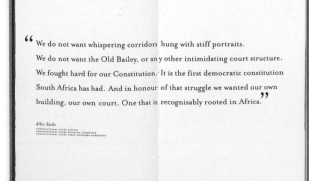

"Go with your heart, park the ego, and always remember, this is never easy."

—Garth Walker

BELOW
The newsletter published by the 4 Museums of Durban, the city's historical and cultural museum precinct, tells stories of the city's history in the design style of the time. Mahatma Ghandi's story reflects Victorian design, and the 1930s flying boats are Art Deco.

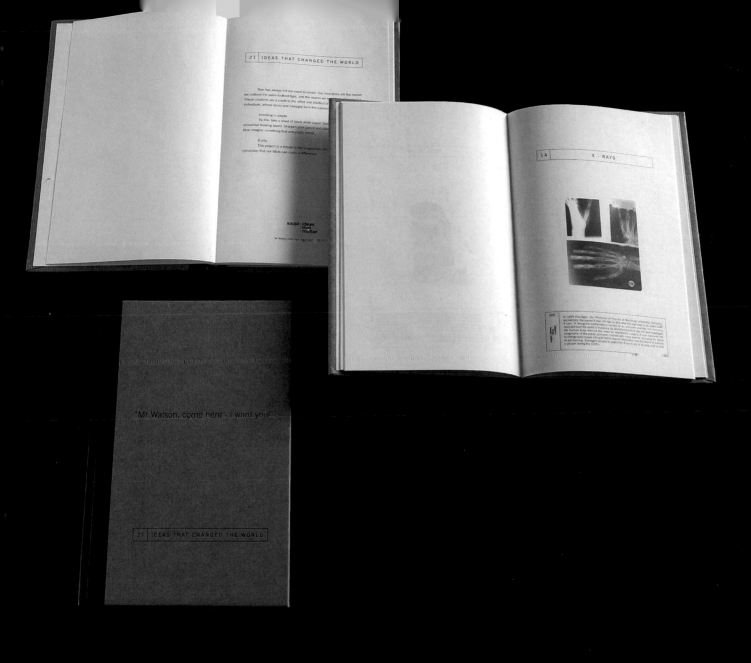

OPPOSITE ABOVE
These booklets, aimed at high-end corporate customers, reflecting Royal Food's approach to healthy executive dining. Walker designed a piece that looked European with a classic visual language.

OPPOSITE BELOW
BPO is Africa's largest logistics, stevedoring, storage, and shipping organization. Walker based the design of this informational brochure on typography and visual imagery and icons that are found in and around the Port of Durban, the company's home base.

ABOVE
This booklet for the South African paper company, SAPPI, is based on "21 ideas that changed the world." Twenty ideas range from X-rays to sewing machines—the twenty-first being the SAPPI Ideas initiative.

WE LIVE HERE.

CALIFORNIA PACIFIC MEDICAL CENTER *A Sutter Health Affiliate*
CALIFORNIA PACIFIC MEDICAL CENTER FOUNDATION
ANNUAL REPORT 2002

ATTENDS DIABETES
SUPPORT GROUP

DONATES ANNUALLY
TO THE FOUNDATION

WORKS NIGHTS IN THE
INTENSIVE CARE UNIT

Caffe Trieste
VALLEJO AND GRANT
SAN FRANCISCO

CHEN DESIGN ASSOCIATES
SAN FRANCISCO, CALIFORNIA, USA

LEFT
Joshua Chen

RECOVERING FROM
ARTHROSCOPIC KNEE SURGERY

TEACHES YOGA TO
HIV-POSITIVE PATIENTS

GETS ANNUAL PHYSICALS

Crissy Field, East Beach
MARINA AND BAKER
SAN FRANCISCO

Sunnyside Elementary
FOERSTER AND FLOOD
SAN FRANCISCO

TOOK ASTHMA

FINGER SAVED THROUGH
MICROSURGERY

GOT NINE STITCHES

For twenty years, Chen Design Associates has created work that expresses the genuine and the necessary, the illuminating and the unexpected. "Almost anyone can shuffle a logo across a slate of different media and call it a campaign," says Chen. "Telling your best story gets your business noticed. Telling it in bold and authentic terms keeps your audience riveted, and loyal." The work is guided by design thinking grounded in the particular needs of each client. Chen Design Associates is committed to a process of collaboration, education, and dynamic invention. Intelligent risk-taking is countered with the skill to build consensus from divergent views. The finished product is about the essence of the client and how what distinguishes them from the pack.

PAGES 180–181
Chen Design Associates'
concept for the California
Pacific Medical Center
annual report demon-
strates how the center is
an integral part of the San
Francisco community. By
using the theme "We Live

Here," Chen reinforced
the notion of California
Pacific Medical Center
as an integral part of the
wellness of the community.
Using panoramic photog-
raphy, the story is told of
how the medical center
is an unseen, underlying

connection shared by
many people going about
their daily lives. Portraits
showcase the experiences
and personalities of
individuals well beyond the
expected titles of patient,
doctor, volunteer, and staff.

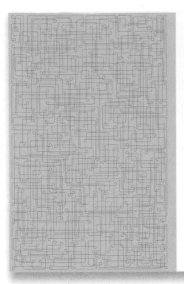

Aarhus Alexandria Amsterdam
Ankara Auckland Baton Rouge
Berango Beverly Hills Boston
Brooklyn Broumana Cambridge
Culver City Durango East
Elmhurst Hixson Hong Kong
Irvington Jakarta London Los
Angeles Ludwigsburg Malvern
Melbourne Mexico City Mogliano
Veneto Muggiò New York City
Oakland Oporto Osijek Paris
Philadelphia Phoenixville Quarry
Bay Reigate Richmond Hill
Roccapietra Saint Augustine San
Diego San Francisco San Jose
Santa Ana São Paolo Seattle
Seoul Singapore Stockholm
Szabadszallas Taichung
City Tokyo Wanchai Victoria
International Design Awards 2007

Contents

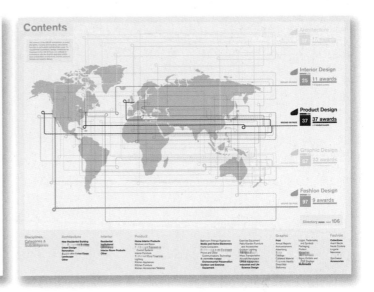

Competitions

IDA exists to recognize, celebrate and promote legendary design visionaries and to uncover emerging talent in architecture and interior, product, graphic, and fashion design.

IN the surf film *Endless Summer II*, two devoted surfers travel to the far reaches of the world to surf some epic waves. The film shows them navigating towering waves with impossible athleticism and grace. Afterwards, they leave their surfboards in the sand.

A moment passes.

from the forest. He smells the oblong object. He noses it. And we thus see a creature from the wild smitten with a piece of wood warped in a way that scintillated the animal to obsession.

We're all creatures who nose up to, sniff and otherwise investigate manmade phenomena. Objects and their design can please us, motivate us, and uplift spirit and heart. Items have power.

Our mission with the International Design Awards is to seek out architecture and design in interiors, products, fashion and graphics that motivate us to curiosity, like the bear, and have the power to elevate. The designers in this book have, at some point, been hit by a creative impulse. The execution may look different; but the search for excellence unifies the book. The selection of winners was difficult, as the standards were rigorous and the competition stiff; and we invite designers worldwide to submit projects in 2008 to be considered for Designer of the Year in this encouraging environment.

We hope you're thus inspired.

James Waugh
Producer
International Design Awards

Student Architect of the Year

Floor Plan: JUNIOR / 1 Bath

www.somagrand.com

ABOVE
Great ideas deserve great design. Soma Grand is the kind of concept that requires impeccable visual communication. The first of its kind in San Francisco, this twenty-two-story residential tower is at the nexus of the city's world-class arts, entertainment, and shopping district. The idea is to provide hassle-free living with someone capable of managing all the details. Chen Design Associates designed the materials to promote these benefits to potential buyers.

NARROWING THE DIVIDE ARTISTS FROM DIVERSE CREATIVE AND CULTURAL BACKGROUNDS MAKE REVEALING CONNECTIONS AS THEY REFRAME IDEAS FROM ONE CONTEXT AND TRANSFORM THEM THROUGH FRESH PERSPECTIVES.

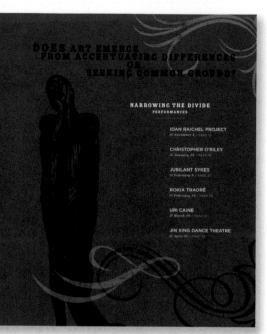

DOES ART EMERGE FROM ACCENTUATING DIFFERENCES OR SEEKING COMMON GROUND?

NARROWING THE DIVIDE
PERFORMANCES

IDAN RAICHEL PROJECT
// November 8 / PAGE 10

CHRISTOPHER O'RILEY
// January 28 / PAGE 16

JUBILANT SYKES
// February 9 / PAGE 21

ROKIA TRAORÉ
// February 16 / PAGE 15

URI CAINE
// March 19 / PAGE 2

JIN XING DANCE THEATRE
// April 28 / PAGE 12

EXTENDING A VISION PLAYING A LEADING ROLE IN ORIGINATING AND DEVELOPING NEW ART, STANFORD LIVELY ARTS HAS COMMISSIONED VISIONARY VOICES TO CREATE NEW COMPOSITIONS AND WILL SHOWCASE THEIR PREMIERES THIS SEASON.

EXTENDING A VISION
PERFORMANCES

PHILIP GLASS, *BOOK OF LONGING*
// October 9 / PAGE 4

ALARM WILL SOUND
featuring a new work by John Adams
// November 20 / PAGE 11

EMERSON STRING QUARTET
featuring a new work by Bright Sheng
// February 6 / PAGE 22

TURTLE ISLAND QUARTET
// February 16 / PAGE 20

WHEN DOES
COLLABORATION
LEAD TO INNOVATION?

WHAT DOES ART
TELL US ABOUT
OURSELVES?

2007 → '08
⇒ /// *performing*
arts season

STANFORD
LIVELY ARTS

WHAT FUELS
CREATIVITY?

CAN ART
INSPIRE CHANGE?

ABOVE
Stanford Lively Arts commissions great artists of our time. Chen Design Associates crafted the content along themes that punctuate the season catalog with powerful messaging and visual rhythm. The quality of the programming is represented by creating a comprehensive look and feel for all their communication materials, including the season catalog, magazine covers, street banners, various direct-mail components, giveaways, and a website.

SHOCK OF THE OLD

De magie van Olivier Messiaen
in 4 concerten

DI 5 FEBRUARI 2008
GROTE ZAAL 20.15 UUR

de doelen   Kaarten bestellen?
010 2171717 of
www.dedoelen.nl

DIE SCHÖPFUNG

Haydn's Meesterwerk

—

Orkest van de Achttiende Eeuw
o.l.v. Frans Brüggen

VR 24 APRIL 2008
GROTE ZAAL 20.15 UUR

de doelen   Kaarten bestellen?
010 2171717 of
www.dedoelen.nl

MISSA SOLEMNIS

Beethoven – Missa Solemnis

—

Hofkapelle Stuttgart en Kammerchor Stuttgart
o.l.v. Frieder Bernius

MA 1 OKTOBER 2007
GROTE ZAAL 20.15 UUR

de doelen   Kaarten bestellen?
010 2171717 of
www.dedoelen.nl

MONTEVERDI'S OPERA
ORFEO

Scenisch in de Grote Zaal
New London Consort o.l.v. Philip Pickett

'Monteverdi as authentic as it gets' – The Observer

MA 19 NOVEMBER 2007
GROTE ZAAL 20.15 UUR

de doelen   Kaarten bestellen?
010 2171717 of
www.dedoelen.nl

Jacques Koeweiden

● **Koeweiden Postma** • Amsterdam, The Netherlands

Koeweiden Postma distinguishes itself through simple and powerful work. Their philosophy is not based on beauty, but on allowing design to be honest and direct communication. Founder Jacques Koeweiden maintains that the goal is to not hide a company's real nature or character behind a façade of obscure or excessive design. This direct approach does not preclude the element of surprise. "We work on intuition and always try to avoid the obvious," he says. "This also follows the fact that we work for clients in both the corporate, cultural, and social sectors. The exchange of experience we get from this keeps us fresh and sharp, and gives more depth to the things we do."

OPPOSITE
The new communication style developed for De Doelen Concert Hall and Congress Centre in Rotterdam profiles the main stage as a place for music for a broad audience. With a program of classical and modern music, jazz, world music, and concerts for children, the concert hall focuses on a wide range of the population requiring a communication style that reaches both traditional and younger target groups, all from different cultural backgrounds.

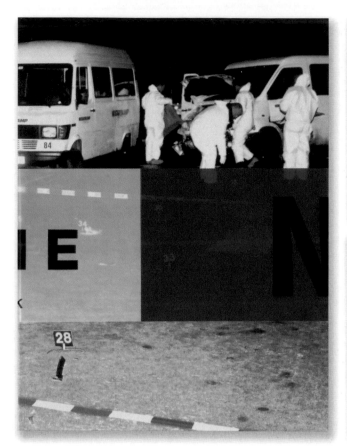

'HET VOELT ALS EEN AANSLAG'

Courage

Koeweiden Postma strives to find the visual presentation that best represents a client's character and message, and is captive and attractive. Koeweiden's favorite projects are the ones made for clients who demonstrate a lot of courage. "It is wonderful when my client and I share the same daring attitude," says Koeweiden.

One of Koeweiden Postma's first projects was a book for the Dutch Design Association BNO, featuring Dutch design agencies and designers. Koeweiden proposed a curved edge for the cover; the client and design team loved the idea. When it came time to produce the piece, however, no printer had the capability to produce the cover. The design team eventually found a producer of beer mats who was prepared to make the cardboard covers. Unfortunately, Koeweiden didn't consider that it is impossible to fold the actual printed cover around the curved cardboard. As a result, the nicely shaped edge of the cover revealed the gray cardboard backing. To solve this, they sprayed the exposed edges of 30,000 books with metallic paint three times, then applied another two layers of varnish by hand.

Large and Small

The format, whether it is large or small, curved or flat, is derived from the concept and the client's wishes. Koeweiden's design for the 2003 Police Annual Report needed space to show the illustrations by Marion Deuchars, hence the larger format of 24½ x 30 centimeters (approximately 9½ x 12 inches). For the 2004 Annual Report, Koeweiden depicted twenty-four hours of police work in a photographic story. This was best presented in a horizontal format. The 2005 Annual Report measures 16 x 21½ centimeters (6¼ x 8½ inches), presents three important cases the police handled in that year, and is meant to be read like a book.

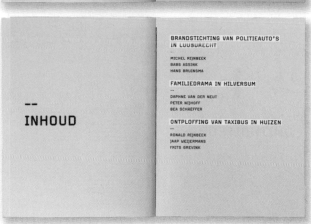

Although the web and digital media have their specific benefits, Koeweiden's work demonstrates that print still has a very important role in corporate communication. The solutions created for Dutch retail chain HEMA use both online and printed brochures to communicate with clients. "The impact of a printed object on the viewer is different than online communications. Printed brochures are for inspiration; the web is for information or dedicated purchases. Print communicates in a different way than the web," says Koeweiden.

Responsibility

Sustainable practices are paramount at Koeweiden Postma. They accept the responsibility to use resources in a sensible way. This includes technical issues such as using FSC-certified nonchlorine bleached paper and ink with low or no volatile compounds. This responsibility also extends to the purpose and design. "We won't waste any paper with bad design or useless printed matter," he says.

Every aspect and component of a solution should be examined and not neglected. Printers in the Netherlands have generally maintained high standards in the area of sustainable practices.

The work maintains a high level of integrity, skill, and power, but Koeweiden's passion is also evident. There is an intangible aspect of every creative endeavor. The emotion and spirit of the creator is typically present. There is a clear difference, for example, between the original Van Gogh painting, *Starry Night*, at the Museum of Modern Art in New York, and a perfect replica by another artist. Koeweiden explains, "I try to get the utmost from an assignment, to work on it with full passion and integrity, and make the most of it. I forget the 'blah blah.' and don't try to be fancy and hip. That is just a thin layer—I look at more than that. In this way, I force myself to look further."

ABOVE
The murder of Pim Fortuyn and several other cases made 2002 a year in which the Gooi en Vechtstreek police force received more press attention than ever. The relation to the press, therefore, was a logical topic for the annual report of the force. The report has the form of a documentary about three dominant events in the past year. Existing images, interviews, and a voice-over of the police chief are the only ingredients of the report.

PAGES 192–193
The annual report for 2003 Gooi en Vechtstreek police force has a somewhat different form in relation to the rest of the series. The personal motivations of the policemen and women lay out the soul of the police force in this report, and by this, the relation of the police with society. British illustrator Marion Deuchars was asked to visualize and illustrate the stories of the police employees.

Maatschappelijke integriteit

Illegale handel algemeen (drugshandel, mensensmokkel, wapenhandel en fraude)
Aantal verdachten in onderzoeks-dossiers illegale handel   4
Overgedragen onderzoeksdossiers illegale handel   1

Zeden algemeen
Aantal verdachten in onderzoeks-dossiers illegale handel   0
Overgedragen onderzoeksdossiers illegale handel   0

Milieu (criminele org.)
Aantal verdachten in onderzoeks-dossiers illegale handel   0
Overgedragen onderzoeksdossiers illegale handel   0

Omvang jeugdcriminaliteit
Aangehouden minderj. verdachten / aangehouden verdachten   476 / 3.923
Aangehouden minderj. verdachten / minderjarigen CBS   478 / 14.263

Wijze van afdoening jeugdzaken
Percentage Halt-verwijzingen minderjarige verdachten   25.16%
Afdoeningen OM minderjarige verdachten   45.79%

Weg algemeen
Aantal bekeuringen   125.075

Snelheid
Aantal bekeuringen   103.005

Alcohol
Aantal bekeuringen   348
Aantal processen-verbaal   739

Gebruik gordel / helm
Aantal bekeuringen   6.189

Rood licht
Aantal bekeuringen   6.476

Weg overig
Aantal bekeuringen   9.057
Aantal processen-verbaal   193

Ondersteuning evenementen (in manuren)
Sport (m.n. voetbal)   1.055
Demonstraties   705
Evenementen overig   12.530
Totaal   14.290

Aantasting openbare orde
Aantal misdrijven   18

Discriminatie
Aantal misdrijven   5

Restcategorie
Aantal misdrijven   82

Ontneming wederrechtelijk verkregen voordeel
Aantal ontnemingsrapportages   33
Aantal afgerapporteerde verdachten in zaken   33
Totaal bedrag aan voorgestelde ontnemingen   621.953

Dienstverlening

Dienstverlening
Functioneren van de politie   5.3
Tevredenheid over contact met de politie   63.9

Bereik en beschikbaarheid
Bereik- en beschikbaarheid   4.0
Spoedeisende meldingen (binnen de norm in %)   92.3

Preventieadviezen
Preventieadviezen bij aangifte (in %)   25.7

Slachtofferzorg
Aantal doorverwijzingen naar Slachtofferhulp / 100 aangiften 9.90
Informatie aan Slachtofferhulp bij aangifte (in %)   29.7

Klachten
Aantal klachten   84

Hulpverlening
Aan personen, aantal meldingen   2.356
Aan instanties, aantal meldingen   616

Overige dienstverlening
Restcategorie meldingen   0

Interne performance

Strafrechtketen
Percentage
Aanhouden/uitreiken   11.64
Doorlooptijd in dagen   56.74
Technisch sepotpercentage   1.56

Marja Visser
Hoofd Personeel & Organisatie

Meditatie

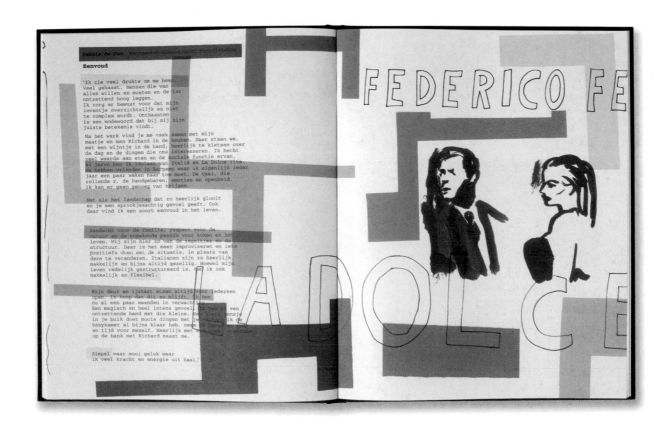

Debbie de Coo

Eenvoud

'Ik zie veel drukte om me heen.
Veel gehaast, mensen die van
alles willen en moeten en de lat
ontzettend hoog leggen.
Ik zorg er bewust voor dat mijn
leventje overzichtelijk en niet
te complex wordt. Onthaasten
is een modewoord dat bij mij zijn
juiste betekenis vindt.

Na het werk vind je me vaak samen met mijn
maatje en man Richard in de keuken. Daar staan we,
met een wijntje in de hand, heerlijk te kletsen over
de dag en de dingen die ons interesseren. Ik hecht
veel waarde aan eten en de sociale functie ervan.
Al jaren ben ik idolaat van Italië en La Dolce Vita.
We hebben vrienden in Bergamo waar ik eigenlijk ieder
jaar een paar weken naar toe moet. De taal, die
rollende r, de handgebaren, emoties en openheid.
Ik kan er geen genoeg van krijgen.

Net als het landschap dat zo heerlijk glooit
en je een sprookjesachtig gevoel geeft. Ook
daar vind ik een soort eenvoud in het leven.

Aandacht voor de familie, respect voor de
natuur en de ongekende passie voor koken en het
leven. Wij zijn hier zo Van de regeltjes en de
structuur. Daar is er meer improviseren en iets
positiefs doen met de situatie, in plaats van
deze te veranderen. Italianen zijn zo heerlijk
makkelijk en bijna altijd gezellig. Hoewel mijn
leven redelijk gestructureerd is, ben ik ook
makkelijk en flexibel.

Mijn deur en ijskast staan altijd voor iedereen
open. Ik hoop dat dit zo blijft. Ik ben
nu al een paar maanden in verwachting.
Een magisch en heel intens gevoel. Ik als een
ontrettende band met die kleine.
in je buik doet mooie dingen met je. Hoewel ik de
babykamer al bijna klaar heb, neem ik af en toe
en tijd voor mezelf. Heerlijk met een boek op strand,
op de bank met Richard naast me.

Simpel maar mooi geluk waar
ik veel kracht en energie uit haal.'

FEDERICO FE
LA DOLCE

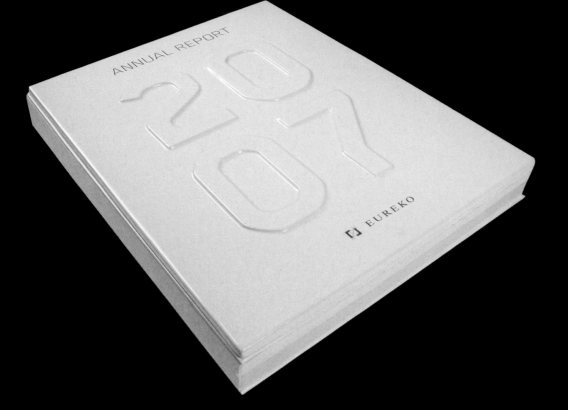

The 2007 annual report
for insurance holding
company Eureko has a
cover made of porcelain.
The ceramic cover on
a small part of the print
run refers to the theme
of the report: "Because
everything you value is
vulnerable." The starting
point for this concept is the
phrase by Dutch poet and
artist Lucebert: "All things
of value are defenseless."

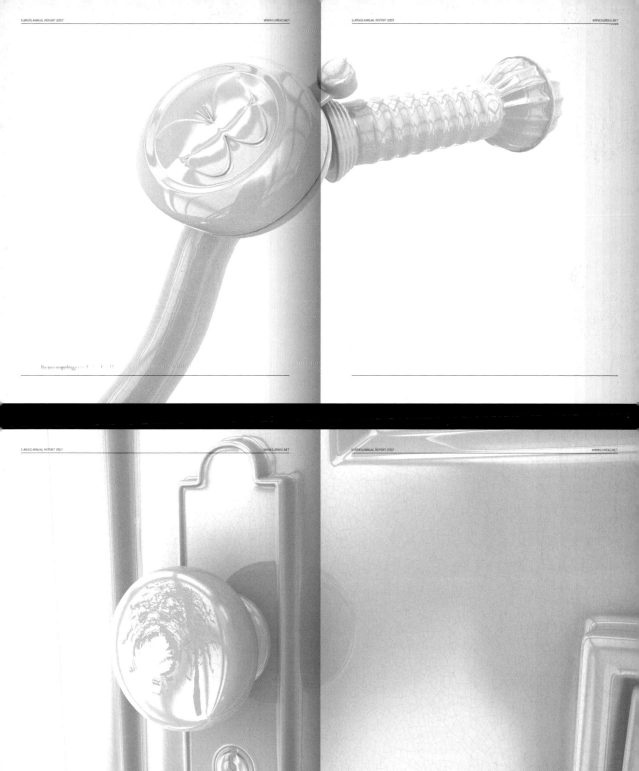

Because everything you value is vulnerable

LEFT, BELOW,
AND OPPOSITE
The design used for the Verslag Ramadan Festival is a combination of Islamic ornamental art and the tradition of Dutch design. When visual communication is aimed at ethnic target groups, a typical response is to use design elements from their "own" culture. This often produces an oversimplified, clichéd, and outmoded result. The aim of the design for the Ramadan Festival is to integrate elements of Islamic design with modern, Western design and create something entirely new. Koeweiden Postma worked to contribute towards integration and better communication with ethnic target groups.

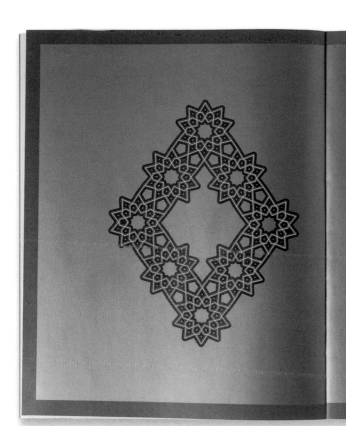

De campagne
in het kort

< 14 verschillende flyers >
< 58.500 flyers totaal >
< 2 posters,oplage van 1.240 >
< 4 weken lang 425 (AO) posters
  verspreid in Amsterdam >
< 15 keer tv spotje op AT5 >
< 1 promoteam 16 promoteamleden >
< 22 digitale aankondigingen >
< 4 digitale nieuwsbrieven >
< 3.616.630 hits op de website >
< 306.717 hits op 5 oktober
  waarvan 22,4% uit het buitenland,
  waaronder 5% uit België >
< 70 links op andere sites >
< 14 persberichten >
< 2 advertenties in het Amsterdamse
  Stadsblad, 10 in de Metro NL,
  1 in Mzine >
< 4.943 emailadressen >
< 5 mailingen per post >
< 1000 T-shirts >
< 96 radiospotje op FunX >

Opening:
in het kort

< 307 bezoekers >
  57% Moslim,43% niet moslim
  (schatting op basis van de
  gastenlijst) >
< 20 journalisten >
< 15 gastsprekers >
< 15 videoboodschappen >
< 12 keer in de media
  (w.o. NOS journaal, RTVNH,
  RTL nieuws, de Telegraaf,
  de Spits en het Parool). >

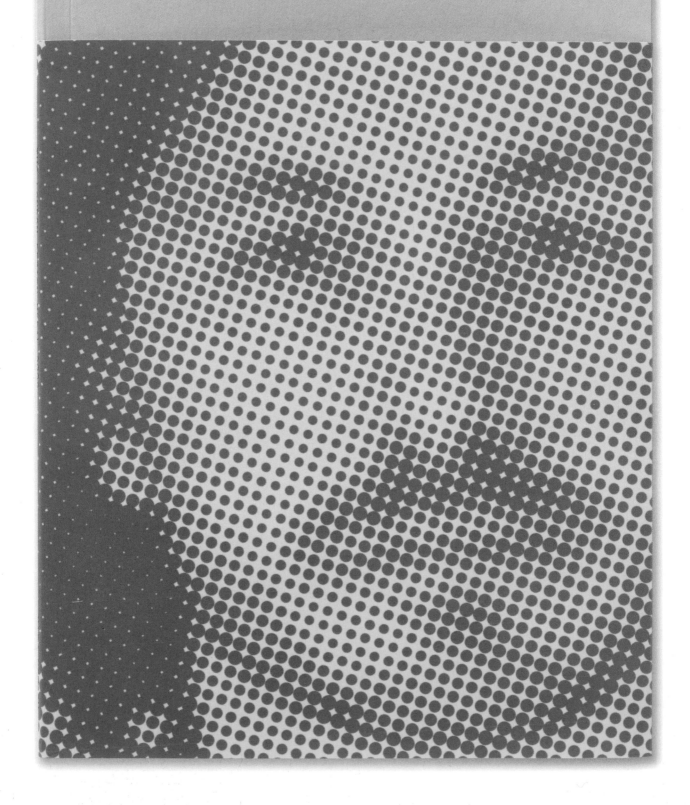

THE LONDON DESIGN MEDAL 2008   MARC NEWSON

Domenic Lippa

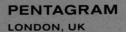

● **Pentagram** ● London, UK

Pentagram partner Domenic Lippa approaches corporate communication with two directives: use common sense and do the job well. Behind this direct approach is a series of questions that is asked at the onset of every project: "What's the job at hand? What needs to be done? What is it that the client wants to communicate? Who does he want to reach? How much can he spend on this? Do we have text only? Do we have images? How much time do we have?" Lippa explains, "What I need to decide then is what should the printed piece look and feel like in order to achieve all that it needs to achieve?"

OPPOSITE AND PAGE 200 The London Design Festival was established to celebrate and promote London as the creative capital of the world and gateway to the UK's world-class creative community. To commemorate Marc Newson's receipt of the London Design Medal, Domenic Lippa designed the award and book presented at the London Design Festival's gala dinner, held at the Phillips de Pury & Company auction house.

_A PORT RAIT

"WHAT I DO HAS
TO BE FUTURISTIC
BECAUSE I WANT WHAT
I DESIGN TO HAVE
A LIFE OF ITS OWN
IN THE FUTURE AND
EXIST WITHOUT ME
IN ITS OWN RIGHT."
_MARC NEWSON

6

The Top 3 Rules

1. When you work on a design always ask yourself:
   Would this printed piece appeal to me? Would
   it convince me?
2. Make it elegant and worthwhile to keep,
   whenever possible.
3. Work with printers who you can trust!

Quality Control

"You're handed a piece of printed communication. You react to it before you even read what it says. If you dislike the look of it, you will throw it in the nearest bin. That's failed communication," says Lippa. He also cites type that is too small and bad printing as factors for failure. Conversely, he mentions the quality of design, the quality of paper, and the quality of the printing and finishing as factors of success. This quality is linked to the media. "Print is part of our culture. On-screen communication can do a lot, but you cannot touch it, and you cannot fold it up and carry it with you, or write on it," he says, "For me, one of the greatest benefits of printed communication is that you can give brochures, books, and posters away as presents." Printed material represents an actual value as opposed to a website that the viewer consumes online and that does not have any tangible worth.

Do No Harm

Given the material and resource issues with printed matter, Lippa addresses sustainability by encouraging the client to maintain small and efficient qualities, reducing page count and size when possible, and making something so beautiful that nobody will throw it away. But he acknowledges that our role as designers does have a negative effect on the environment. "We cannot *not* harm the environment, but we can try to cause as little damage as possible," he explains. Once again, the issue of high quality is at the heart of his philosophy. "Find a printer who is willing to help you achieve great results, and who can teach you the secrets and tricks of the trade," he advises. This collaboration for Lippa has produced solutions that are successful aesthetically, sustainable, and produce actual results.

ABOVE
Time & Territory is a book published by the landscape architecture and urban design firm J&L Gibbons to celebrate their twenty-first anniversary.

The book's design reflects the interplay between analysis, intuition, thought, process, and sustainability that is characteristic of J&L Gibbons' work.

tenth issue of Circular

International conflict pulls countries apart and we continue to degrade the planet as the suffering of our fellow men and women continues unchecked. At the same time developments in technology make information more accessible than ever before, bringing unthinkable benefits to us all. Whilst in some countries diseases have been eradicated, in others food mountains tower over the starving. We have witnessed the fall of Communism, the fall of Thatcherism and the rise of New Labour and we still cannot seem to repeat the sporting successes of '66.

CIRCULAR 11 contains work from the five speakers we have had during the last year. Chronologically we began with the maverick and experimental *Graphic Thought Facility*. This was followed by the precision and detail of *North*. In contrast *Alan Fletcher* proved that you didn't have to be young to provide the inspiration. *SEA* were next up, continuing the modernist theme. We then finished with *Vince Frost* who is one of the few designers able to straddle the 'old school' ideas-based approach with a sensitivity to the final look of the design.

ABOVE AND PAGES
204–205
Typographic Circle is a
nonprofit organization
formed in 1976 to bring
together anyone with an
active interest in type
and typography. For issue
fifteen, Lippa developed
a new logo, creating a
roundel resembling a *C*
out of the words Circular
Fifteen. The magazine
features articles on design
and typography contributed
by the Typographic Circle's
network of members and
collaborators, such as an
Alan Fletcher retrospective
written by Quentin Newark
and an extract from Richard
Hollis' book on Swiss
typography.

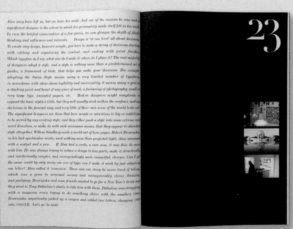

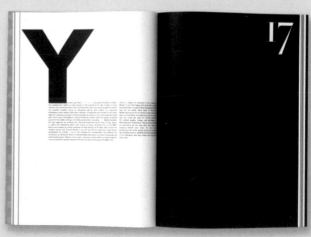

"There is only one way to go about this: Do the right thing!"
—Domenic Lippa

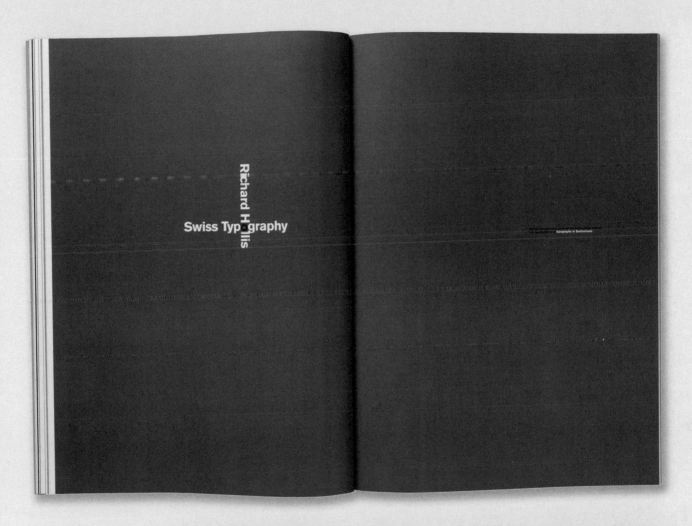

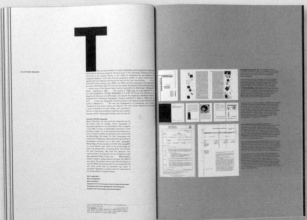

Michael Vanderbyl

Vanderbyl Design • San Francisco, California, USA

There are designers who change styles to accommodate each client, and there are designers who adhere to one strict visual language, regardless of the project. Michael Vanderbyl addresses each client and project uniquely without imposing a preset style. But he does not schizophrenically switch from one visual genre to another. He is able to synthesize the best qualities of a client, translate the message clearly, and produce communications that yield practical results. And Vanderbyl does more. With a level of craft and form-making skill unsurpassed in the industry, he adds a layer of quality and brilliance to each project. He is unafraid of being accused of embracing grace and understands that human beings have an innate desire to find beauty.

OPPOSITE AND PAGES 208–209 "Design Does Matter" is a collection of essays on design for Teknion Furniture Systems. The development of this pair of books has its roots in a "back to business in the post-dot-com era" approach. The books reflect a less radical, more classic sentiment. The essays emphasize the importance of design and highlighting Teknion Furniture Systems' commitment to design.

05

75 million

If only one percent of all paper faxes sent in North America each year were sent elec[...], we'd save more than 75 million trees.

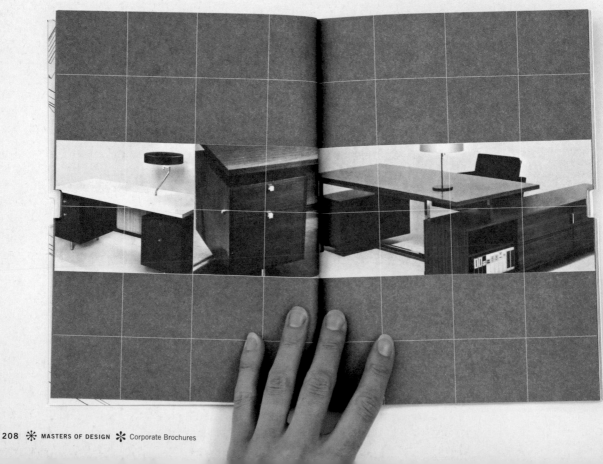

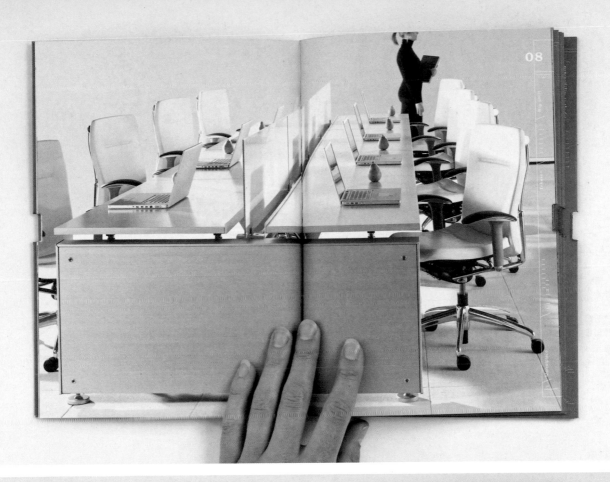

...s suitable for a wide range of applications. Space division up to 66 inches high and 96 inches wide
...nventional workstations appear architectural. District can be used to create traditional office layouts
...arying degrees of enclosure and privacy. In addition, vertical surfaces of District create walls that support
...-worksurface storage cabinets.

"Books represent a moment in time. People love books and keep them. People treasure books, not websites."

—Michael Vanderbyl

Since Vanderbyl Design's establishment in 1973, the firm has evolved into a multidisciplinary studio working across media including print, packaging, signage, interiors, showrooms, retail spaces, furniture, textiles, and fashion apparel. The media is secondary to the message, and each project starts with an exploration into the substance of a client. "Essentially, we find out who the client is, and then communicate that message," says Vanderbyl. "We strive to communicate what qualities make the client unique. We also make sure that the client can first defend the message and, secondly, that they can live up to it." One of the most damaging attributes a brand can have is the perception of mistrust. Making exaggerated claims or promoting flawed products will only lead to failure.

Clarity

"Our most basic goal is to provide clarity. Clarity is an integral part of any solution," says Vanderbyl. Reaching that goal requires learning about the client, the products, the audience, and all other facts that impact the brand. One of the first things Vanderbyl Design does when they begin working with a client is to actually try to buy their product. Vanderbyl explains, "Doing this tells us a lot about the issues that truly need to be addressed. I don't automatically assume that design is the answer." The solution may have more to do with the product itself, or the customer service experience, or a multitude of other issues. A good logo and brochure will not solve every problem.

Media and Audience

In order to pair the right medium with the right message, Vanderbyl looks at the problem being solved. What audience are we talking to? How does this audience access information or perceive the brand message? "Much of our work is creating communication and branding programs for designer products," says Vanderbyl. "We're always trying to find the best communication method for a particular client's needs. So we are open to a variety of platforms." In recent years, Vanderbyl has found that clients are requesting more than printed matter. In addition to the traditional communication vehicles, he is now using additional media, websites, or an email blast to communicate to increasingly complex audiences.

Vanderbyl's appreciation for print is evident in the attention paid to printing, paper, and format. "I think there is a reverence for print. We're not going to eliminate print completely. Print allows you to go at your own pace, without plugging anything in," he notes. "Print commemorates something. It's special. Print stops a moment in time regarding a product, service, or event." He is noted for the high quality of hand-bound books his firm has created. Vanderbyl says, "Books represent a moment in time. People love books and keep them. People treasure books, not websites. Digital media is great because it's instantaneous, but it will never replace ink on paper."

ABOVE AND OPPOSITE Vanderbyl has taught at the California College of the Arts (formerly California College of Arts and Crafts) for over thirty years. He is currently the Dean of Design. The CCAC catalog explores themes of "blue sky" open ideation, art as the center of a creative person's life, and the personal experience. Clear information is presented with personal statements from students. This accomplishes the task of linking the individual to the viewer, and proves the authenticity of the message. The catalog's strong graphic language does not recede and allow the images of art to dominate.

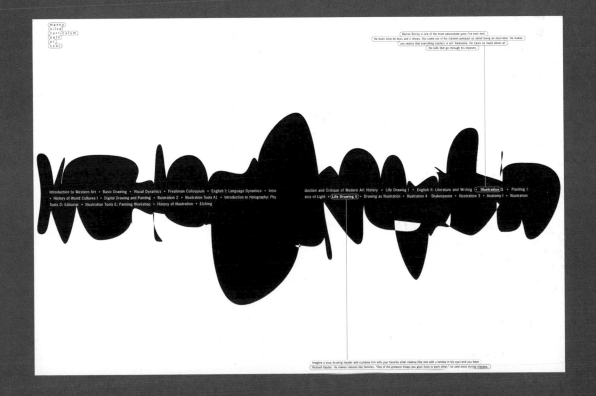

"I left a pharmacy program in Michigan to explore San Francisco's burgeoning multimedia industry and underground techno-music scene. A deejay by night, I was becoming an expert on design software at a digital-media trade publication during the day. Shortly after, I enrolled at CCAC to pursue a formal design education—one that offered the theory, history, and conceptual process I was seeking. Now I have an important critical perspective on the work I produce. Away from CCAC, I work at Post Tool, a digital studio run by my mentor and friend, David Karam. As a result of my work thus far, I was featured in I.D. Magazine's 'Forty Designers Under Thirty' issue. After CCAC, I want to continue pursuing my interests in music and design—finding innovative ways to synthesize the two."

manny
silva
curriculum
path
at
ccac

Barron Storey is one of the most passionate guys I've ever met. He loves what he does and it shows. You come out of his classes pumped up about being an illustrator. He makes you realize that everything matters in art. Awesome. He cares so much about all the kids that go through his classes.

Introduction to Western Art • Basic Drawing • Visual Dynamics • Freshman Colloquium • English I: Language Dynamics • Introduction and Critique of Modern Art History • Life Drawing I • English II: Literature and Writing • Illustration 1 • Painting I • History of World Cultures I • Digital Drawing and Painting • Illustration 2 • Illustration Tools A1 • Introduction to Holography: Physics of Light • Life Drawing II • Drawing as Illustration • Illustration 4 • Shakespeare • Illustration 3 • Anatomy I • Illustration Tools D: Editorial • Illustration Tools E: Painting Workshop • History of Illustration • Etching

Imagine a wise drawing master and combine him with your favorite older relative (the one with a twinkle in his eye) and you have Richard Gaytor. He makes classes like families. "One of the greatest things you guys have is each other," he said once during classes.

ABOVE AND RIGHT
The Beauty and Nuance
promotion demonstrates
the printability and quality
of Mohawk Superfine.
The promotion is produced
with one small booklet
bound onto a larger one.
The promotion links the
most beautiful objects
with the highest caliber
of printing on the paper.
It has a clear message
and demonstrates the
product's capabilities
in a form that becomes
a coveted artifact.

PLATE
05

PEDRO GUITERREZ
ROBERTO MELOZO PEREZ
DANIEL TREJO MARAVILLA
RAMON LOPEZ CASTRO
[CLOCKWISE TOP LEFT]
GRAFTERS

MAY 30, 2005

ABOVE AND RIGHT
Materials for Scarecrow
Wine celebrate the people
involved in the making
of the product. The name
and icon, a scarecrow,
pay homage to the found-
ing winemaker, J.J. Cohn,
who had been the chief
of production at MGM
during the making of *The
Wizard of Oz*. Vanderbyl
combines classical
typography, high-quality
images, and printing with
a casual and playful tone.

OPPOSITE
The Annual Napa Valley Wine Auction, sponsored by the Napa Valley Vintners Association, is staged yearly at Meadowood Resort. Since 1981, the auction has raised more than $36 million (£23 million). In 2001, it generated $7.6 million (£4.9 million) for health care, housing, and youth development nonprofits in Napa County.

Vanderbyl's materials for the 22nd Annual Napa Valley Wine Auction uses the theme of a festive fair, Cirque du Vin. The dinner featured five chefs from New York's Le Cirque restaurant. Images and patterns recall European fairs but are mixed with contemporary elements and unexpected combinations. The size difference between the cover and interior of the book references a beloved artifact.

Vanderbyl's confident and gracious demeanor would suggest a process with no complications, but the reality is different. "Our biggest challenge is getting clients on board with what we're trying to do. Getting them to understand how design can help them accomplish their goals," he says. Many clients tend to think about their organization or product only from their own point of view, not from the perspective of the people they are trying to speak to and persuade. "This is not about personal taste. It's not about the designer. It's about who the client is trying to reach," says Vanderbyl.

Gestalt

Vanderbyl's work is typically clean, spare, and maintains classical proportions and typography. For him, excess is the hallmark of failed communications. Too much information, and none of it clear, will doom a piece. Other factors that lead to failure are a lack of a general gestalt. This is evident in projects with multiple messages conveyed in a variety of styles. Invariably, the predominant message is hidden and lost in the design. Vanderbyl says, "As designers, it's our job to make complex things accessible."

There are also almost always budgetary restrictions. "In all my years of experience it seems that we are always up against various budget issues. We do a lot of 3-D and environmental work, and we never have enough money in

the budget," he explains. This is not apparent in any of Vanderbyl's solutions. The finished piece, regardless of budget, is designed with the highest level of craft, and is married integrally to its format and medium.

Translating the same message from print to web, environment to product is an ongoing challenge that grows increasingly complex as new technologies are created. Vanderbyl explains, "My favorite client project is when I get to do everything—take an idea and express it in lots of media. It ensures we'll be successful because it's consistent and therefore more effective. Too many cooks can really spoil the broth." Throughout the process of every project, Vanderbyl works to keep everything close to the original vision. He maintains a clear message, not by replicating the exact same form like a rubber stamp, but by designing pieces from a specific point of view and tone. "Our business model is to develop long-term relationships with our clients," says Vanderbyl, "Because of this, we are doing everything for the client and maintaining consistency."

Resolving these issues leads to successful projects. "The more successful I make my clients, the more successful I am," explains Vanderbyl. He has followed the philosophy of doing good work for good clients since the firm's establishment. He says, "Remember that we are the keepers of the written word and the spoken word as well. Always work to communicate the word."

This simple two-color project is part of the reidentification of the ArtCouncil. The chipboard-covered, perfect-bound brochure focuses on imparting the message of the organization: to support emerging artists, arts education, and discourse about art. The letter from the president and founder is laid out over eight pages with type and placement varying on each page. This approach visually engages the reader to the text and emphasizes the importance of these words. The body of the brochure describes the ArtCouncil's philosophy and programs, highlighted with a timeline diagram of twentieth-century art movements and quotes.

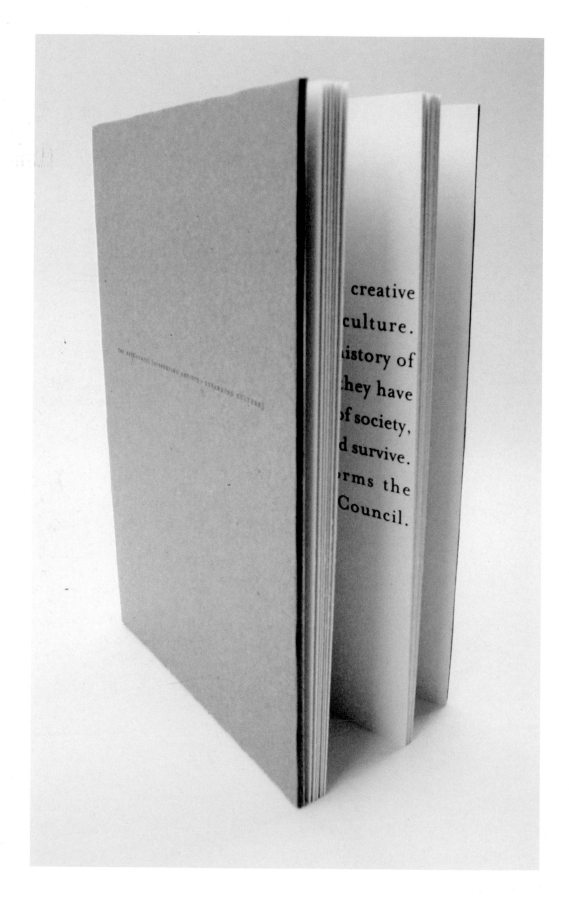

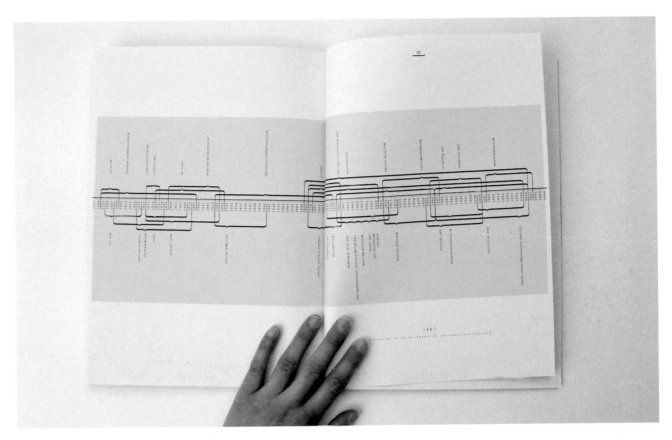

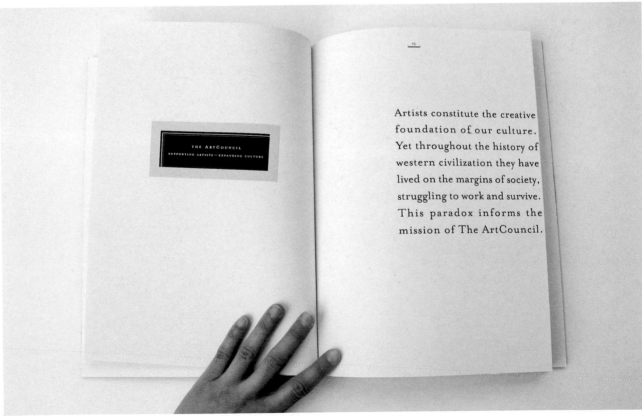

THE ARTCOUNCIL
SUPPORTING ARTISTS — EXPANDING CULTURE

Artists constitute the creative foundation of our culture. Yet throughout the history of western civilization they have lived on the margins of society, struggling to work and survive. This paradox informs the mission of The ArtCouncil.

ABOVE AND OPPOSITE
Communications materials
for noted interior designer
Barbara Barry reflect
Barry's design ethos
of modern classicism.
Vanderbyl begins with
the elements of classic
book design: symmetrical
typography, classic
typefaces, one color
palette, and typographic

elements. He works with
these forms, but injects the
unexpected and modern.
The forms do not sink into
fussy or decorative. They
openly ignore the rigid
classical rules: fonts are
mixed, letterspacing is
explored, the symmetry
of the page is violated.

PLATE no. 3

DOMESTIC BLISS

Celebrate each day the beauty of the ordinary and the humble, as well as the costly and the rare. Simple white dishes or soft linens neatly stacked on a shelf can be a cause for quiet joy.

◊

PLATE no. 4

BEAUTIFUL PROCESS

Design is a process that begins perhaps with a recollection, an image, of things seen and loved. The image becomes a sketch and then a model, refined and perfected until the finished object approaches the imagined ideal.

◊

DIRECTORY OF CONTRIBUTORS

1 **2 Fresh**
Can Burak Bizer
Maslak Beybi Giz Plaza, K:26
Istanbul 34396 Turkey
90.0.212.335.2734
www.2fresh.com

2 **Blok Design**
Vanessa Eckstein
Sombrerete 515 #1
La Condesa 06170 Mexico DF
Mexico
+5255.5515.2423
www.blokdesign.com

3 **Cahan & Associates**
Bill Cahan
171 2nd Street, 5th Floor
San Francisco, CA 94109 USA
415.621.0915
www.cahanassociates.com

4 **Chen Design Associates**
Joshua Chen
649 Front Street, Third Floor
San Francisco, CA 94111 USA
415.896.5339
www.chendesign.com

5 **Doyle Partners**
Stephen Doyle
1123 Broadway, 6th Floor
New York, NY 10010 USA
212.463.8787
www.doylepartners.com

6 **Essex Two**
Joseph and Nancy Essex
2210 W. North Avenue
Chicago, IL 60647 USA
773.489.1400
www.sx2.com

7 **Carin Goldberg Design**
Carin Goldberg
16 2nd Street
Brooklyn, NY 11231
718.522.4026
www.caringoldberg.com

8 **Grant Design Collaborative**
Bill Grant
111 E. Marietta Street
Canton, GA 30114 USA
888.479.8280
www.grantcollaborative.com

9 **Alexander Isley Inc.**
Alexander Isley
9 Brookside Place
Redding, CT 06896 USA
203.544.9692
www.alexanderisley.com

10 **Koeweiden Postma**
Jacques Koeweiden
Danzigerkarde 9c
1013 AP Amsterdam
The Netherlands
+31.20.612.19.75
www.koeweidenpostma.com

11 **Kuhlmann Leavitt, Inc.**
Deanna Kuhlmann-Leavitt
7810 Forsyth Boulevard, 2 West
Saint Louis, MO 63105 USA
314.725.6616
www.kuhlmannleavitt.com

12 **Larsen**
Tim Larsen
7101 York Avenue South
Minneapolis, MN 55435 USA
952.835.2271
www.larsen.com

13 Methodologie
Janet DeDonato, Dale Hart
& Anne Traver
720 Third Avenue, Suite 800
Seattle, WA 98104-1870 USA
206.623.1044
www.methodologie.com

14 Mister Walker
Garth Walker
461 Berea Road Durban KZN
PO Box 51289
Musgrave Road 4062
South Africa
+27.31.2771855
misterwalkerdesign.com

15 Pentagram, Berlin
Justus Oehler
Leibnizstrasse 60
10629 Berlin, Germany
+49.0.30.27.87.61.0
www.pentagram.com

16 Pentagram, London
Domenic Lippa
11 Needham Road
London W11 2RP
United Kingdom
+44.0.20.7229.3477
www.pentagram.com

17 SamataMason, Inc.
Dave Mason & Kevin Krueger
101 South First Street
West Dundee, IL 60118 USA
847.428.8600
www.samatamason.com

18 Shinmura Design Office
Norito Shinmura
Seibido Bldg.4F, 6-7-8 Ginza, Chuoku,
Tokyo 104-0064 Japan
81.3.3572.5042
www.shinmura-d.co.jp

19 Steinbranding
Guillermo Stein
El Salvador 5675
Buenos Aires C1414 BQE
Argentina
54.11.4011.5555
www.steinbranding.com

20 Tank Creative Intelligence
Jim Antonopoulos
30 Lalor Street
Port Melbourne
VIC 3207
Australia
+61.3.9646.2909
www.tankstudio.com.au

21 Tomorrow Partners
Gaby Brink
2332 Fifth Street
Berkeley, CA 94710 USA
510.644.2332
www.tomorrowpartners.com

22 Vanderbyl Design
Michael Vanderbyl
171 Second Street, 2nd Floor
San Francisco, CA 94105 USA
415.543.8447
www.vanderbyldesign.com

23 VSA Partners
Jamie Koval & Dana Arnett
1347 S. State Street
Chicago, IL 60605 USA
312.427.6413
www.vsapartners.com

BIBLIOGRAPHY

Adams, Sean, Noreen Morioka, and Terry Stone. *Logo Design Workbook.* Gloucester, MA: Rockport Publishers: 2004.

Chermayeff, Ivan, Tom Geismar, and Steff Geissbuhler. *TM: Trademarks Designed by Chermayeff & Geismar.* New York: Princeton Architectural Press, 2000.

Chermayeff, Ivan, Tom Geismar, and Steff Geissbuhler. *Designing.* New York: Graphis Press, 2003.

Dondis, Donis A. *A Primer of Visual Literacy.* Cambridge, MA: MIT Press, 1973.

Fella, Edward. *Letters on America.* New York: Princeton Architectural Press, 2000.

Friedman, Mildred, Editor. *Graphic Design in America: A Visual Language History.* New York: Abrams, 1989.

Gardner, Bill, and Cathy Fishel. *LogoLounge: 2,000 International Identities by Leading Designers.* Gloucester, MA: Rockport Publishers, 2003.

Halberstam, David. *The Fifties.* New York: Ballantine Books, 1994.

Hall, Peter, and Michael Bierut, Editors. *Tibor Kalman, Perverse Optimist.* New York: Princeton Architectural Press, 1998.

Heller, Steven. *Paul Rand.* London: Phaidon Press, 1999.

Hess, Dick, and Marion Muller. *Dorfsman & CBS.* New York: American Showcase, 1987.

Jacobson, Egbert, Editor. *Trademark Design.* Chicago: Paul Theobald, 1952.

Jaspert, W. Pincus, W. Turner Berry, and A. F. Johnson. *The Encyclopaedia of Type Faces.* London: Blandford Press, 1953.

Johnson, Michael. *Problem Solved: A Primer in Design and Communication.* London: Phaidon Press, 2002.

Kirkham, Pat. *Charles and Ray Eames: Designers of the Twentieth Century.* Cambridge, MA: MIT Press, 1995.

Meggs, Philip B. *A History of Graphic Design* (Third Edition). New York: Wiley, 1998.

Meggs, Philip B. *Type and Image: The Language of Graphic Design.* New York: Wiley, 1992.

Moss, Marie Y. *Hello Kitty Hello Everything! 25 Years of Fun.* New York: Abrams, 2001.

Müller-Brockmann, J. *The Graphic Artist and His Design Problems.* New York: Hastings House, 1961.

Neuhart, John, Marilyn Neuhart, and Ray Eames. *Eames Design: The Work of the Office of Charles and Ray Eames.* New York: Abrams, 1989.

Pentagram. *Pentagram Book Five.* New York: Monacelli Press, 1999.

Rosen, Ben. *The Corporate Search for Visual Identity.* New York: Van Nostrand Reinhold, 1970.

Tuckerman, Nancy, and Nancy Dunnan. *The Amy Vanderbilt Complete Book of Etiquette.* New York: Doubleday, 1995.

Wheeler, Alina. *Designing Brand Identity: A Complete Guide to Creating, Building, and Maintaining Strong Brands.* New York: Wiley, 2003.

Young, Doyald. *Logotypes & Letterforms: Handlettered Logotypes and Typographic Considerations.* New York: Design Press, 1993.

ABOUT THE AUTHOR

COLOPHON

Sean Adams is a partner at AdamsMorioka with offices in Beverly Hills and New York. He has been recognized by every major competition and publication, including *STEP*, *Communication Arts*, *Graphis*, AIGA, The Type Directors Club, the British Art Director's Club, and the New York Art Director's Club. A solo exhibition on AdamsMorioka was held at The San Francisco Museum of Modern Art, and Adams has been cited as one of the forty most important people shaping design internationally in the ID40.

Sean is the national president and past national board member of AIGA and former president of AIGA Los Angeles. He is a Fellow of the Aspen Design Conference, as well as AIGA Fellow. He teaches at Art Center College of Design. Sean is a frequent lecturer and competition judge internationally. Adams is the coauthor of *Logo Design Workbook*, *Color Design Workbook*, and *Masters of Design: Logos & Identity*. AdamsMorioka's clients include ABC, the Academy of Motion Picture Arts and Sciences, Adobe, Gap, Nickelodeon, Sundance, Target, USC, and the Walt Disney Company.

This book was designed in the Spring of 2009 by Sean Adams and Monica Schlaug. The principal typeface is Trade Gothic, designed by Jackson Burke, produced by Mergenthaler Linotype in 1948. Headlines use Akzidenz Grotesk, designed by H. Berthold Berlin Typefoundry in 1896.